NEA
EARLY CHILDHOOD
EDUCATION SERIES

Educationally Appropriate Kindergarten Practices

Bernard Spodek
Editor

A NATIONAL EDUCATION ASSOCIATION
P U B L I C A T I O N

Printing History
First Printing: September 1991

Note

The opinions expressed in this publication should not be construed as representing the policy or position of the National Education Association. Materials published by the NEA Professional Library are intended to be discussion documents for teachers who are concerned with specialized interests of the profession.

Library of Congress Cataloging-in-Publication Data

Educationally appropriate kindergarten practices / Bernard Spodek, editor.
　　　p.   cm. — (NEA Early childhood education series)
　　Includes bibliographical references.
　　ISBN 0–8106–0350–0
　　1. Kindergarten—United States—Curricula.   2. Kindergarten—United States—Activity programs.   I. Spodek, Bernard.
　　II. Series: Early childhood education series (Washington, D.C.)
　　LB1180.E38   1991
　　372.19—dc20   91–10647
                                                                    CIP

CONTENTS

The Advisory Panel

Richard P. Ambrose, Assistant Professor of Teacher Development and Curriculum Studies, Kent State University, Ohio

Janice M. Banka, Teacher-Director of Early Childhood Education Program, Oak Park School District, Michigan

Frances B. Moldow, Elementary School Teacher (retired), Fair Lawn, New Jersey

Sandra L. Moran, Kindergarten Curriculum Developer, Morongo Unified School District, Twentynine Palms, California

Mary Regas, Elementary School Teacher, Brunswick, Ohio

C. Stephen White, Assistant Professor of Early Childhood Education, The University of Georgia, Athens

INTRODUCTION

by Bernard Spodek

Kindergarten was first introduced into the American public school system about 120 years ago. Since that time, there has been continuing discussion about the role kindergartens should play in the education of young children and about the content of kindergarten education (5).* For many years the kindergarten was viewed as the first educational experience for children outside their home. In these earlier days, few children were enrolled in nursery schools or day care centers, and even enrollment in kindergarten was limited to a minority of five-year-olds.

In this period the kindergarten served as a vestibule for the elementary school. As young children came into the kindergarten they needed to be socialized into their new role as students, learning how to function in the social institution of the school that included children and adults in roles that were different from those in their families. The purpose of a school was also different from that of a family; children needed to learn to become goal-oriented in a way they had not been before. The year of kindergarten education served as a low pressure socialization period, providing children with many experiences they might not have had before school. As a result, children could begin the primary grades on a more level playing field.

The situation began to change in the late 1960s. Alterations in the lives of young children in our society caused the kindergarten to be viewed differently (6). An increasingly large number of children had some form of planned educational

---

*Numbers in parentheses appearing in the text refer to the References at the end of the chapter.

5

experience before beginning elementary school. With more full-time working mothers, especially mothers of young children, there was a dramatic increase in enrollments in child care centers.

Research in the early 1960s on the causes of poverty led to the creation of the Head Start program. This community action program was originally part of President Lyndon Johnson's War on Poverty. Over the years, Head Start and similar programs designed for children from poor families have shown themselves be effective ways of helping children succeed in school. Children from such programs were retained in grade less often, fewer of them were recommended for placement in special education classes, more of them completed high school, and a host of other long-term positive educational outcomes were identified (1, 2).

At the same time that enrollment in prekindergarten programs was expanding, so were enrollments of five-year-olds in kindergarten. Twenty five years ago, most five-year-olds did not attend kindergarten. Today, kindergarten education has become practically universal. In many states kindergartens are offered on a full-day, everyday schedule; only a few years ago almost all kindergartens were either half-day, everyday, or all day, part-week. In addition, an increasing number of states are supporting prekindergarten programs in the public schools for children ages three and four, and sometimes even younger.

Presently, more than half of the children entering kindergarten have already been in some sort of educational program. Because of this, kindergartens no longer need to function as vestibules for the school. Children have, for the most part, already been socialized into the educational system before they arrive in the elementary school. In addition, since all five-year-old children are expected to attend kindergarten, kindergarten can be better integrated into the regular school experience of all children. As a result, schools and teachers are again asking what the role of the kindergarten should be. Since a socializing kindergarten no longer serves a valid purpose, should

6

not kindergarten become more academic? Should the kindergarten become more like first grade, with academic subjects like reading, writing, and arithmetic taught there just as in the grades that follow?

Unfortunately, kindergartens have become more academic in some communities. Most children entering kindergarten have already spent a year in typical early childhood activities, such as singing, story telling, block building, dramatic play, and the like. It was felt that they would be bored with a continuation of that. In addition, young children today have a greater access to information about the world than they had in the past. All these reasons served to support the need for an enriched kindergarten program for contemporary five-year-olds. With no other idea of how to enrich the program, the curriculum of the first grade was imported into the kindergarten.

Such a move has had significant consequences. In many communities, a large number of children entering kindergarten were not ready to learn the content of the first grade using the traditional method of the first grade. As a result, many communities have raised the entrance age to kindergarten. In the past, children entering kindergarten had to reach the age of five by December 1 or January 1. Many communities now require that children already be five-years-old at the start of the school year. Some children were also not completing the new kindergarten curriculum successfully. Transition classes to first grade have been established and school systems are increasingly screening children before they are allowed to enroll in kindergarten. Five-year-old children who are felt to be "not ready" for kindergarten may be asked to defer enrollment for a year or be placed in "developmental kindergartens" and provided with a second year of kindergarten education.

Many of these practices have been severely criticized as having negative consequences for young children (3, 4). Yet they arose as a consequence of heightened expectations for children, a not entirely negative educational goal.

Kindergarten programs can be rich in intellectual content without using workbooks or depending on paper-and-pencil learning activities. Children can learn language and thinking skills at the same time as they interact informally with a wide range of materials and people. The key is for the teacher to understand the goals that we wish to accomplish in the kindergarten, to understand the ways in which young children think and learn, and to be aware of the range of learning opportunities that can be created for young children.

In developing sound kindergarten programs, teachers need to avoid thinking about school content in the narrow sense of teaching each subject area directly and separately. Rather than offering lessons to children, teachers need to offer activities that allow children to access the content of subject areas while doing other things as well. Teachers should use knowledge of subject matter areas as an analytic tool to identify the potential educational outcomes of kindergarten activities rather than to delineate the concepts to be taught through some form of direct instruction.

In the chapters that follow, the contributors present the basis for educationally worthwhile activities. This relates not only to the issue of developmental appropriateness but also to the educational worth of kindergarten goals and the activities that are used to achieve those goals. The contributors also provide examples of how kindergarten programs can be organized and worthwhile learning presented to young children. Long-term projects or units are seen as useful vehicles of instruction. Organizing teaching around topics or themes helps teachers present complex ideas within their contexts so that young children can more easily understand them. This organization avoids the linear teaching found in some classrooms. Thinking of the curriculum as a series of webs helps the teacher keep track of the relationship of activities to each other and to the goals to be achieved.

The organized activities presented here relate to community organization, as in studying the community bus system, health and nutrition, language and literacy, and multicultural education. These are only a few examples of many topics or themes that can be approached in the kindergarten. These materials are designed for kindergarten teachers. They combine theoretical discussions with examples of practical application. Finally, there is a discussion designed to help kindergarten teachers create meaningful learning experiences for children in their classrooms. The book has been written in the hope of helping teachers create content-rich, activity-oriented, developmentally appropriate, and educationally worthwhile kindergarten programs for their children.

REFERENCES

1. Collins, R. C. "Headstart: An Update on Program Effects." *Newsletter of the Society for Research in Child Development,* Summer 1983.

2. Lazar, I., and Darlingtom, R. "Lasting Effects of Early Education." *Monograph of the Society for Research in Child Development* 47 (1982). Serial No. 195.

3. Meisels, S. J. *Developmental Screening in Early Childhood: A Guide.* Washington, D.C.: National Association for the Education of Young Children, 1989.

4. Shepard, L. A., and Smith, M. L. "Synthesis of Research on School Readiness and Kindergarten Retention." *Educational Leadership* 44 (1986): 78–86.

5. Spodek, B. "Needed: A New View of Kindergarten Education." *Childhood Education* 49 (1973): 191–95.

6. Zimiles, H. "The Social Context of Early Childhood in an Era of Expanding Preschool Education." In *Today's Kindergarten: Exploring the Knowledge Base, Expanding the Curriculum,* edited by B. Spodek. New York: Teachers College Press, 1986.

1. WHAT SHOULD WE TEACH KINDERGARTEN CHILDREN?

by Bernard Spodek

As kindergarten education has expanded during the past several years, there have been pressures to change the kindergarten curriculum. Some schools have extended their elementary program down, often including what had been the first grade instruction. Since most children now enter kindergarten with prior early childhood educational experience, the traditional play-oriented kindergarten curriculum was seen as denying them a valid educational experience. It was also felt that beginning academic instruction one year earlier would increase the probability that the children would learn to read.

A great many early childhood educators and parents have become concerned with such changes. Many fear that children are being given academic instruction prematurely and inappropriately. In response, the National Association for the Education of Young Children (NAEYC) published a set of criteria for developmental appropriateness of programs for young children (2). In fact, while developmental appropriateness is an important criteria in determining the value of an early childhood program, other criteria are equally important.

CHILD DEVELOPMENT AND EDUCATION

How does one test for the developmental appropriateness of a program? The test cannot be universal, since there is no universal agreement about what constitutes human development. One can only judge developmental appropriateness within a particular theory of development. Conceptions of development are embedded within specific theories and there are several such theories competing with each other in the field.

Lawrence Kohlberg and Rochelle Mayer (8) placed developmental theories and educational theories within educational ideologies. The *romantic* ideology reflects the view of development as maturation and education as the unfolding of inner virtues and abilities. The *cultural transmission* ideology conceives of education as passing knowledge, skills, values, and social and moral rules from one generation to the next. Behaviorism provides the psychological principles for a technology of education offering a variation on direct instruction within this stream. The *progressive* ideology views education as helping the child achieve higher levels of development through structured, though natural, interactions with the physical and social environment.

The idea of education as the attainment of higher levels of development reflects this relationship between human development and education that has resulted in a conception of the teacher as a child development specialist. This ideology is consistent with constructivist conceptions of development and education that have been based upon Piaget's work.

These three approaches reflect different relationships between child development and education. Determining whether a program is developmentally appropriate first requires identifying the ideological stream within which the program is embedded. *Romantic* programs usually have embedded within them a maturational concept of readiness. Children may be given developmental tests to determine their developmental level and thus their readiness for a program. If they are judged not to be ready, they are often withdrawn and allowed to mature before being enrolled in a program. In *cultural transmission* programs, children might be tested to determine whether they have the prerequisites for learning what is expected of them in a program. If they do not, then they will be moved to a lower instructional level and instructed in their identified areas of deficiency. In *progressive* programs, children will be provided with experiences

11

to help them move on to higher levels of development, or the program will be reconstructed so that the children will be able to grasp the knowledge required of them in a more appropriate way.

As noted, each conception of development will allow teachers to assess children's level of development to match the educational program to the children's competencies and abilities. Each conception of development—each ideology—has different consequences for the child, however. A teacher who accepts a maturational view of development might withhold a child in a grade or even request that the child not enter school if that child is considered to be developmentally delayed. In contrast, a teacher who accepts a cultural transmission view of development would probably provide that same child with a series of remedial exercises to teach the child those things that have not already been learned. A progressive teacher, again with the same child, would present that child with problematic situations to resolve—situations that would be challenging without being frustrating—to help move the child to more mature ways of functioning.

There are also differences between developmental theory and educational theory. Fein and Schwartz (4) have suggested that theories of development are universalistic and minimalist, describing what is considered a normal course of growth and change within an environment with a minimal core of features. In contrast, educational theories are particularistic and maximalist, dealing with practice related to particular individuals in specific settings aimed at maximizing the benefits of deliberate interventions. In addition, developmental theory views change in the individual as a result of multiple influences, while educational theory looks essentially at the influence of particular practice on individuals. Though educational theory and developmental theory inform each other, one cannot be derived from the other. Several quite different early childhood education programs have been created that are related to particular developmental theories; each one is different from the rest. Forman and Fosnot (6), for example, have analyzed a number of unique early childhood curricula that are labeled "Piagetian" to identify their similarities and differences. There are probably more differences among the programs studied than there are similarities. These differences arise because each program developer focused on a different aspect of Piagetian theory for inspiration. In addition, more than developmental theory underlies any educational program.

A knowledge of child development is important for all kindergarten teachers. Such knowledge allows teachers to anticipate what kindergarten children are capable of learning as well as the process by which they learn, a process that is different from that of adults and even older children. It also helps them understand that the range of abilities, skills, and understandings found among the children in a kindergarten class is a normal reflection of individual differences in children. Any class can be expected to have a difference of 12 months between the oldest and the youngest child. The range of developmental differences might be even broader. Understanding development, the teacher will accept these differences and adapt the program for each child, appropriately challenging those at higher levels of development as well as those at lower levels.

Although developmental theory can be viewed as a resource to the early childhood curriculum, it is not its basic source (10). Biber (1) has suggested that the starting place for an educational program "should be a value statement of what children ought to be and become" (p. 303).

THE CONTENT OF KINDERGARTEN PROGRAMS

There is no doubt that the process of educating young children is closely related to their level of development. Knowledge of child development helps educators understand what young children are capable of knowing, and how children gain and validate knowledge at a particular stage in their

13

development. But what children ought to learn at the kindergarten, or any other level of education, is not solely determined by what they are capable of learning. I have suggested that while child development research and theory can serve as an important resource in developing an early childhood curriculum, the level of a society's technology and the society's cultural values are equally important (11).

Hirsch (7) argues forcefully that there are some things that all children in a society ought to know. Children need this knowledge to understand the discourse of the society and to participate in its processes. Hirsch uses schema theory—which is helping educators understand how children come to abstract meaning from the written page as they read—to undergird his arguments.

While one can argue about what specifics children need to know to be "culturally literate," few will argue that there is some common knowledge that individuals must assimilate to participate fully in the social discourse and processes of a community. In our pluralistic society, most of us belong to more than one community simultaneously; thus, each of us must acquire more than one body of cultural knowledge.

Making the content of early childhood education explicit does not require that all children learn the same thing or that there be a single standard early childhood curriculum. There are many ways that the appropriate content of an early childhood curriculum can be identified. We need to begin to openly and consciously define what is considered to be the appropriate content of education for kindergarten children. In doing this, we need to use other criteria besides developmental appropriateness.

It might be helpful in beginning this process to look at early childhood education programs that diverge from what we view as the norm and that reflect different traditions from our own. This would allow us to see other possibilities besides those that traditionally have existed in our schools. It would also allow us to become more aware of the assumptions about kindergarten education that we take for granted. Let me briefly describe two alternative programs: kindergarten programs in the People's Republic of China and those provided in Jewish schools in America. China has a very different early childhood program from our own, based on different educational assumptions. Jewish early childhood education programs in America are also different and can provide another alternative.

Kindergartens in China

Contemporary Chinese kindergartens serve children ages three through six. Their program, modeled after Soviet kindergartens, includes six curriculum areas: music, language, mathematics, physical education, art, and general knowledge (science and social studies). Opportunities for play are provided and meals, snacks, health inspections, naps and informal activities are included daily. Kindergartens, like all schools and businesses in China, operate six days a week.

The curriculum is taught through daily lessons, with three- to four-year-olds having one or two 15-minute lessons daily, four- to five-year-olds having two 20–25-minute lessons, and five- to six-year-olds having two or three 25–30-minute lessons daily. Direct instruction is used with teachers lecturing to children while using teacher-made teaching aids to illustrate the concepts presented. Children sit attentively and quietly around tables, often with their hands behind their backs, listening to the lessons before they participate in related activities (13).

Chinese kindergarten educators, like their American counterparts, are concerned that their programs be developmentally appropriate. However, the Chinese concept of developmental appropriateness is quite different from our own and the primary concern is with the subjects. Kindergarten lessons, while simpler and designed to be more interesting to young children, are no different in kind from those offered to older children and youth. Care is taken, however, not to place undue stress on the children, and the lessons are kept short and interesting.

Chinese kindergarten educators have a strong sense of what the content of the programs should be and what knowledge the children should acquire. While no one could argue that Chinese kindergarten educators are less concerned for the welfare of their children than we are, many American kindergarten educators probably would view Chinese kindergartens as placing a heavy burden on young children.

American Jewish Early Childhood Programs

A study of what should be taught in Jewish early childhood programs provides a very different perspective on the early childhood curriculum. Feinberg (5) studied the curriculum choices of Jewish nursery schools and kindergartens to identify what Jewish early childhood educators want children to know. Rather than consulting the child development literature, traditional Jewish knowledge was used as a curriculum source.

These early childhood schools serve a specific population of Jewish-American children, a group with distinct traditions, values, and other cultural elements. While there is much that these programs have in common with other American early childhood programs, much of their content is unique. They have a serious concern with socializing children into a specific ethnic and religious culture, thus seeking a specific form of cultural literacy. The curriculum for these young Jewish children has to be explicitly identified and consciously taught. These children could not acquire this cultural knowledge base through informal community interactions or contacts with the mass media, by which many of our cultural elements are transmitted.

Children in these early childhood classes are expected to learn the roots of Jewish culture. While the content of these programs is different from standard American kindergarten programs, their methods, materials, and organization are quite similar. The programs are rich in content, yet they are also developmentally appropriate and thus capable of being learned by the children.

American Kindergarten Programs

Even a cursory review of the Chinese kindergarten shows that its curriculum constructs are different from those of American kindergartens. Each is based on a different theoretical orientation, with different standards for what constitutes appropriate educational activities. The concepts of developmental appropriateness used by Chinese and American early childhood educators are also different. But American Jewish early childhood educators hold the same theoretical orientation as their non-Jewish counterparts. The goals and content of the Jewish early childhood programs are different, though each is based on the same considerations of developmental appropriateness because they are based on a different culture.

The Jewish early childhood educators have made their educational goals and purposes explicit as have their Chinese counterparts. One cannot find the same explicit statement of goals and purposes for American early childhood programs as for the other programs mentioned here. Nowhere is there a statement of what all children in kindergarten or preschool are expected to learn or know as a result of their educational experiences outside of statements of academic readiness or statements in support of children's personal development.

In spite of this, there seems to be an implicit agreement among early childhood educators about what knowledge is to be transmitted to young children in kindergarten. Standard American kindergarten programs teach about the American way of life, about the English language, about America, and about American values and attitudes. The day-to-day curriculum experiences offered in early childhood programs relate to the American way of life. The knowledge we want young children to acquire about that way of life is embedded in the books we read

17

to them, the stories we tell, the songs we sing, the experiences we offer, and the relations we nurture among children and between children and adults.

One of the most important elements of all kindergarten programs is language. Literacy education for young children is being viewed as increasingly significant. However, literacy skills are only part of the language learning provided to young children. We teach about the content, structure, and function of the American language to both bilingual and monolingual children. We also share rich oral and written traditions of children's literature and poetry, folk stories, and fairy tales.

Many of the holidays we celebrate with children in school—Columbus Day, Thanksgiving, President's Day, Martin Luther King Day, and so on—relate to American history and American traditions. These are celebrated in school to instill a sense of American peoplehood. These celebrations and the learning related to them help all children, whatever their cultural background and cultural heritage, develop a sense of identity with the American culture, while not necessarily denying their own personal family background and culture. While these elements are an implicit part of our kindergarten programs, because they are unarticulated, they are—unfortunately—unstudied.

Since ours is a pluralistic society, made up of many ethnic, cultural, and racial groups, a variety of subcultures must contribute to the cultural base of the school curriculum at every educational level, including kindergarten. While there is much that we all must learn in common with one another, there is great diversity in what individual groups might want their children to know. A balance must be struck in the schools between having all children learn things in common and having alternative goals and content for children as individuals and as members of different ethnic, geographic, and cultural groups. The fact of our multiculturalism requires that we learn about other cultures as well as our own, so that the common core of cultural knowledge

18

we want young children to gain should include knowledge representative of minority as well as majority cultures. Thus holidays celebrated by subcultures in American society may also be shared with others. Teachers should be careful, however, that all significant cultural groups are represented in these celebrations, not just those cultures reflected in a particular class of children.

EXPLICATING THE KINDERGARTEN CURRICULUM

If we are to be concerned about what kindergarten children ought to learn, then we need to make explicit the expectations that should underlie our curriculum. A concern for developmental appropriateness alone is obviously inadequate. We need to establish additional criteria for judging what should be taught in kindergarten.

Making the content of kindergarten programs more explicit will not make it less developmentally appropriate. These two characteristics of programs are not mutually exclusive. Besides developmental appropriateness, the values of our culture and the nature of the knowledge children need in order to function competently in our society should determine the content of kindergarten programs (12). Respect for the rights of others, kindness, sensitivity to the needs of others, for example, are basic values of our culture that we wish to nurture through the kindergarten program. The ability to communicate with others and to work cooperatively with others are skills that children must acquire to function adequately in our society. These are among the many skills we should teach in kindergarten. We can identify many other values, skills, and understandings to be taught in kindergarten upon which we can agree. These goals of kindergarten education can be made explicit and programs can be judged in terms of what is taught and the degree to which it is taught well.

19

Some early childhood educators are attempting to make kindergarten program content more explicit. Elkind (3) has recently addressed the issue of what to teach in early childhood education. He has suggested that early childhood teachers should begin to teach young children the content, the concepts, and classification of the different disciplines, such as science, social studies, and history. Young children also should be taught different colors, shapes, and sizes. They should learn to match, categorize, discriminate, and order things according to the similarities and differences of their attributes. Elkind has also suggested that the most appropriate vehicle for educating young children is classroom projects.

Programs that result from ideas such as Elkind's will be consistent with those suggested some time earlier in *New Directions in the Kindergarten* (9). This book, written more than two decades ago, proposed that kindergarten curricula be based on key ideas or concepts from various fields of knowledge. These key ideas could be used to test the intellectual worth of kindergarten content. Activities integrated into units or projects would be designed to be developmentally appropriate.

In rethinking the criteria we use for determining what to teach kindergarten children, we need to use the intellectual value of what is taught as one of the criteria for selecting program content, along with such criteria as developmental appropriateness, utility, and consistency with the values of society. When all these criteria are used to determine what to teach young children, better early childhood programs will be developed and selected.

CONCLUSIONS

Early childhood educators need to reconsider the assumptions they hold about what constitutes a worthwhile program for young children. In doing this, these programs would become educationally, as well as developmentally, appropriate for today's young children.

Kindergarten programs must be concerned with helping children learn the student role as they begin their careers in the public schools. Children in kindergarten must learn the basic values of our society. Some of the values they should develop relate to the importance of academic learning and of becoming competent in basic literacy and mathematical skills. This requires that children develop basic academic skills. But attaining such skills is not enough; kindergarten children must also become independent seekers of knowledge and creative thinkers.

If kindergartens are to improve, educators must design programs that do more than simply prepare children for later schooling. Young children should be provided with programs that help them assimilate the values of our society and that teach significant content. Kindergarten programs need to be evaluated, not only in terms of their developmental appropriateness, but also in relation to their educational worth to the children taught and the communities served. Only when that content is made explicit can it be evaluated as to its effectiveness, its worth, and its practicality.

REFERENCES

1. Biber, B. *Early Education and Psychological Development.* New Haven: Yale University Press, 1984.

2. Bredekamp, S. *Developmentally Appropriate Practice in Early Childhood Programs Serving Children from Birth Through Age 8.* Expanded ed. Washington, D.C.: National Association for the Education of Young Children, 1987.

3. Elkind, D. "Early Childhood Education on Its Own Terms." In *Early Schooling: The National Debate,* edited by S. L. Kagan and E. F. Zigler, 98–115, New Haven: Yale University Press, 1988.

4. Fein, G., and Schwartz, P. M. "Developmental Theories in Early Education." In *Handbook of Research in Early Childhood Education,* edited by B. Spodek, 82–104. New York: Free Press, 1982.

5. Feinberg, M. P. "Placement of Sectarian Content for Jewish Nursery Schools and Kindergartens in the United States." Ph.D. diss. University of Maryland, College Park, 1988.

6. Forman, G., and Fosnot, C. T. "The Uses of Piaget's Constructivism in Early Childhood Education Programs." In *Handbook of Research in Early Childhood Education,* edited by B. Spodek, 185–211. New York: Free Press, 1982.

7. Hirsch, E. D., Jr. *Cultural Literacy: What Every American Needs to Know.* Boston, Houghton Mifflin, 1987.

8. Kohlberg, L., and Mayer, R. "Development as the Aim of Education." *Harvard Educational Review* 42 (1972): 449–96.

9. Robison, H. F., and Spodek, B. *New Directions in the Kindergarten.* New York: Teachers College Press, 1965.

10. Spodek, B. "What Are the Sources of Early Childhood Curriculum?" In *Early Childhood Education,* edited by B. Spodek, 81–91. Englewood Cliffs, N.J.: Prentice-Hall, 1973.

11. ____. "What Constitutes Worthwhile Educational Experiences for Young Children." In *Teaching Practices: Reexamining Assumptions,* edited by B. Spodek, 1–20. Washington, D.C.: National Association for the Education of Young Children, 1977.

12. ____. "Development, Values and Knowledge in the Kindergarten Curriculum." In *Today's Kindergarten: Exploring Its Knowledge Base, Extending Its Curriculum,* edited by B. Spodek, 32–47. New York: Teachers College Press, 1986.

13. ____. "Chinese Kindergarten Education and Its Reform." *Early Childhood Research Quarterly* 4 (1989): 31–50.

2. DEVELOPING AN INTEGRATED UNIT FOR KINDERGARTEN

by Patricia Clark Brown

INTRODUCTION

Kindergarten teachers need to decide how to organize their programs and what content to include. One way to organize kindergarten programs into meaningful structures is to use units or projects. Often kindergarten teachers organize instruction around themes, typically lasting for about a week, with separate topics for each day's arts and crafts activities. Units, on the other hand, involve in-depth studies of a topic and help children develop concepts and skills through the integration of many areas of learning around a topic. Units may last two weeks or more. Because units are more than just a reason for the day's craft activity, the topic should be worth studying.

CHOOSING AN APPROPRIATE TOPIC

There are a number of criteria to consider in choosing a worthwhile topic. The criteria used here come from a variety of sources (e.g., 5, 7, 8, 9, 11):

Is the topic appropriate for the age and developmental abilities of the children? Kindergarten teachers will need to choose concepts and skills that are appropriate for the group of children with whom they are working. The children must be able to handle the conceptual material they are expected to learn. In working with groups of children, however, teachers need to be aware of the range of levels of development and abilities that can be found among the children. Children in a single kindergarten class will typically range a full year in chronological age. The range of developmental levels may be even greater, however, since children develop at different rates. Even within a single child, the rate of development will not be constant, but will be characterized by fits and spurts. Thus, the kindergarten teacher needs to be concerned not only with what is appropriate for five-year-olds in general, but also with what is appropriate for each child in the class.

Developmental appropriateness also applies to the *way* in which a topic is studied. The methods used to teach children must be consistent with how particular children come to know about the world, how they gather information, and how they operate upon that information as they create their own knowledge.

Are the children likely to be interested in the topic? The teacher can introduce topics or select them from interests expressed by the children. Teachers, however, do not have to wait for children to express an interest in a particular topic. They can stimulate interest through field trips, visits by resource persons, materials brought to class, or the use of pictures, videotapes, filmstrips, or books.

Does the topic relate to children's lives? When choosing a topic, it is important for teachers to consider the particular group of young children with whom they are working and the backgrounds of these children. A unit on farming and farm animals is appropriate for children who have firsthand experience with farms or who have access to a farm. Such a unit might be less appropriate for young children living in the city with no opportunity to visit a farm. Conversely, a unit on museums might be appropriate for children in a city where museums are available, but would have little value to children remote from museums.

Does the topic consider the values and culture of the community and of society? To relate the topic to the children's values, beliefs, and experiences, teachers should consider the communities of the children with whom they work. At the same time, some topics will allow teachers to incorporate ideas and activities from different cultures.

Does the topic have the potential for in-depth and long-term learning across a variety of domains or subject areas? Worthwhile topics encourage in-depth study and serve as a means through which concepts and skills can be developed. A good topic will provide opportunities for children to learn mathematics, language and literacy, science, and social studies. It will also allow children to become actively involved in gathering information and constructing their own knowledge. Firsthand learning experiences are important, along with opportunities for children to use what they experience in dramatic play, experiments, discussions, reading and writing, and activities involving construction. In addition, a good unit can often be extended to include learning about related topics.

Are there advantages to studying this topic in school as opposed to elsewhere? Teachers might want to consider whether this is a topic that children are likely to learn about at home or through a community or religious organization. Given the great amount that children are expected to learn and the limited time for school learning, teachers might want to focus more on unit topics that are less accessible to the children out of school. Holidays are an example of a topic that may not need in-depth study at school if children learn a great deal about them at home. This does not mean that teachers should not include holiday activities in the kindergarten curriculum, but that they need not be part of a long-term unit. On the other hand, teachers who have children in their classrooms from many different cultures may want to involve the children in a topic on holidays so that they can learn more about each other's cultures.

Is the topic useful or worth knowing about? Teachers need to consider whether the topic helps children better understand the world around them and whether it promotes the development of knowledge, skills, and attitudes on which later learning will be built.

EXAMPLE: A UNIT ON FOODS

This example of a unit on foods illustrates how teachers can integrate many areas of the curriculum into a unit. This particular unit was chosen using the criteria already discussed:

1. There are many concepts under the broad topic of foods that would be appropriate for young children to learn.

2. Food is an integral, important part of every child's life—not only nutritionally, but socially as well. Most social gatherings include food, and many special foods are prepared and eaten during holidays and celebrations. Thus, children are interested in food and how it directly relates to their lives.

3. The topic allows for the development of skills and concepts in many areas of the curriculum, including mathematics, language arts, science, and social studies. It provides opportunities for children to become actively involved in learning through dramatic play, experiments, writing, field trips, and construction. In addition, the topic offers many possibilities to extend learning into different areas. Children might learn more about how plants grow, how food is packaged, or how fish are caught.

4. Ideas and activities from different cultures can be easily incorporated into the unit. The similarities and differences in foods from various cultures and foods featured in special events, such as holidays, might be explored.

5. The topic offers children the opportunity to learn new concepts and understandings. They can learn about where food comes from, different types of food, nutrition, customs involving food, and how food is

prepared—all of which will help them better understand their world.

6. Although food is something that children have
   experience with every day, most children will not have
   the opportunity to learn food-related concepts, such
   as where food comes from or how it is processed, from
   home experiences. Therefore it is a topic that could be
   usefully studied at school.

Narrowing the Focus—Creating a Concept Map

Once a topic is chosen, it is important to narrow the
focus and determine what new concepts and ideas the children
will be learning. One way to do this is by creating a concept map.
The teacher, alone or with the children, can brainstorm, listing
all the possible ideas related to the topic. An example of a concept
map for the topic of foods is presented in Figure 1. From this
concept map the teacher, or teacher and children, should decide
what ideas are most interesting and relevant to the children in the
particular classroom. Some of the ideas may not be interesting to
some young children or may be too far removed from their
experiences to have any relevance. Teachers also need to consider
the practicality of investigating certain ideas—there may be some
that would be very difficult for teacher and children to do.

After choosing the areas of interest, the teacher might list
the concepts on which the children will focus. A list of concepts
for the unit on food might include:

1. We get our food from plants and animals.

2. Sometimes we make our own food from raw
   ingredients; at other times it is made at a factory and
   we buy it in a package, can, jar, or frozen.

3. We prepare food in different ways to eat it (food can
   be eaten raw, cooked, frozen, or dried).

27

Figure 1
Concept Web for "Foods We Eat"

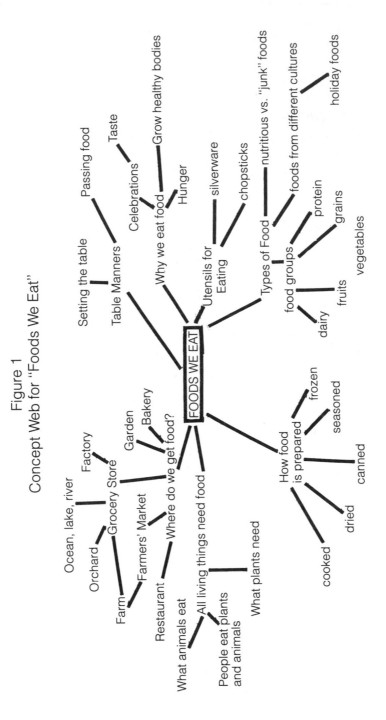

4. We need food to grow and keep our bodies healthy.

5. There are different kinds of food—some food is good for you and some is not as good.

This list includes only some of the possible concepts on which a class could focus. Each teacher or class may have a slightly different list, depending on children's interests and environment, and on the teacher's goals. The list will not cover all the ideas in the map. The map serves as a starting point—a way to identify all the possibilities. Teachers (and children) need to choose from these possibilities those ideas that best fit the interests, abilities, and experiences of the children in that particular classroom. A teacher might narrow the focus of the topic even further. A unit dealing only with where food comes from might include enough ideas and activities to last for quite a while.

Integrating the Unit into the Curriculum

The next step in developing the unit is to incorporate learning from each area of the curriculum (e.g., science, language arts, mathematics, the creative arts). A variety of kindergarten materials and play areas such as blocks, dramatic play, and sand and water tables should be used.

At the beginning of a unit the teacher stimulates children's interest and helps them gather information that would be useful in furthering their understandings. One way to expand the children's experiences and gather information is by going on a field trip. For the unit on food, the field trip might be to a grocery store, a farm or an orchard, a food processing factory, a farmers' market, a restaurant, or a bakery. While field trips are excellent for introducing children to a unit of study, it may not be possible or desirable to take a field trip for each unit. Teachers can also stimulate interest and expand children's knowledge through books, films, and resource persons.

After an introduction to the topic, related activities and experiences can be developed. The children can be encouraged to reconstruct what they have seen on the field trip or what they have learned from a book, film, or visitor to the school. After a trip to the grocery store, for example, the teacher and children might arrange the dramatic play area to re-create the grocery. The children can bring empty boxes and cans from home to stock the shelves. They can put prices on their store goods, and the teacher can provide a cash register and pretend money. A scale in the area can be used for weighing produce. Paper, pencils, and markers should be available for making grocery lists and signs for the store. If the trip is to a restaurant, the dramatic play area can include tables and chairs for diners, menus, pencils and pads for taking orders, dress-up clothes, and pretend food, along with a cash register and pretend money. Children might build a counter for a fast-food restaurant or an assembly line for a factory. It is important, however, that young children have a chance to experience whatever it is that they are going to be re-creating.

Learning concepts and skills in science, social studies, language arts, and mathematics occurs as the teacher and children engage in such activities. Children learn science and mathematics concepts and skills as they measure, plan, construct their store, count food items, "pay" for groceries, and weigh produce. Learning in language arts occurs as the children encounter new vocabulary related to the topic, discuss what they will need for their store, and make signs and lists. Children learn concepts in the area of social studies as they find out how food gets to the store, what people who work in a store do, and how it all relates to their lives. Figure 2 is a curriculum web (see Corwin, Hein, and Levin [4]) that shows how learning in different subject areas is interconnected within one activity (re-creating a grocery store in the classroom) in a unit on foods.

Learning in all curriculum areas can be expanded when other classroom activities are included. For example, the teacher can provide a variety of delivery trucks or farm accessories in the

Figure 2
Curriculum Web for Grocery Store

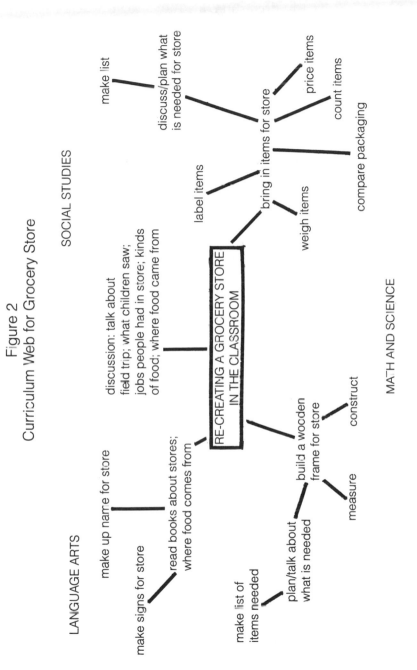

LANGUAGE ARTS

SOCIAL STUDIES

MATH AND SCIENCE

make up name for store

make signs for store

read books about stores;
where food comes from

make list of
items needed

plan/talk about
what is needed

measure

construct

build a wooden
frame for store

RE-CREATING A GROCERY STORE
IN THE CLASSROOM

discussion: talk about
field trip; what children saw;
jobs people had in store; kinds
of food; where food came from

weigh items

bring in items for store

label items

compare packaging

count items

price items

discuss/plan what
is needed for store

make list

block area so that children can construct a town where produce from the farm is delivered to the store. Books, both fiction and nonfiction, about the topic should be made available. Children can write stories and draw pictures about their field trip. Sometimes songs or poems related to the topic will add meaning to what the children are learning. Teachers should plan for a variety of activities that will promote learning in all subject areas when developing a unit of study. The Appendix provides a few activities teachers might consider for a unit related to foods.

Spinning New Units from the Original

As teacher and children study a particular topic, certain ideas will turn out to be more interesting than others. As a result, some ideas will be dropped quickly while others will be pursued in depth, generating new ideas. Not all children have to be involved in exploring the same idea. There will be many areas of interest in any given topic, and small groups of children or individuals can pursue those areas in which they are most interested.

As children explore a topic, their interests will inevitably expand to include other related topics. For example, if the focus of the unit is on where food comes from, the children might become interested in oceans and want to find out more about plants and animals that live in the ocean. If the focus is on nutrition and growing healthy bodies, children might become interested in how they have grown since they were younger, which could lead to a unit on babies. Teachers can pick up on the interests children exhibit at any time during a unit of study and use these to develop new units.

Evaluation

The approach to learning described here does not lend itself to evaluation by standardized tests. This does not mean, however, that there are no ways teachers can know what children have learned during a unit or how they are progressing throughout the year.

One of the best ways to document children's learning is to create a portfolio for each child that includes samples of various kinds of work. Books children have made, paintings and drawings, and group and individual stories about trips and activities can all be included to provide concrete examples of what children have been working on and how they have progressed. Each work sample should be labeled by date. The teacher can see how each child has progressed by comparing earlier work with later work. Talking to children individually and in small groups can also provide teachers with specific information about what understandings children have of a particular concept. Tape recordings of stories and discussions, and photographs, too, can document children's progress.

In addition, teachers can observe children's activities and assess their learning by using checklists or anecdotal records. Spodek, Saracho and Davis (12) present examples of anecdotal records, structured observations, semantic differential scales, and checklists that teachers can develop for assessing children's learning. As teachers collect this information, they can compile a record of each child's progress. They can use this information to determine children's progress toward the goals established for each child by comparing what children are doing at a particular time with what they have done previously.

CONCLUSION

Kindergarten teachers often feel that they have to choose between providing a rigidly structured academic curriculum, complete with workbooks and dittoes, and a kindergarten program that focuses on free play and socialization with little attention paid to learning in content areas. They may feel that the academic curriculum ensures that children will learn in kindergarten and will be prepared for the primary grades. While they often feel that free play and socialization are necessary components of a program for young children, they may be concerned that such activities are less powerful learning tools for the kindergarten. Teachers should not have to choose between academics and socialization or between learning and play. All these aspects of an appropriate kindergarten curriculum can be combined into a flexible, responsive program. A unit approach to organizing kindergarten activities can provide for the development of new concepts and skills in a variety of areas, while giving children the opportunity to interact with one other, to explore, to play, and to create meaning out of their world.

REFERENCES AND RESOURCES

1. Bredekamp, S. *Developmentally Appropriate Practice in Early Childhood Programs Serving Children from Birth Through Age 8. Expanded ed.* Washington, D.C.: National Association for the Education of Young Children, 1987.

2. Brown, J. *Curriculum Planning for Young Children.* Washington, D.C.: National Association for the Education of Young Children, 1982.

3. Chenfield, M. *Creative Activities for Young Children.* New York: Harcourt Brace Jovanovich, 1983.

4. Corwin, R.; Hein, G.; and Levin, D. "Weaving Curriculum Webs: The Structure of Nonlinear Curriculum." *Childhood Education* 52 (1976): 248–51.

5. Dearden, R. F. *Theory and Practice in Education.* London: Routledge and Kegan Paul, 1984.

6. Flemming, B., and Hamilton, D. *Resources for Creative Teaching in Early Childhood Education.* 2d ed. New York: Harcourt Brace Jovanovich, 1990.

7. Katz, L., and Chard, S. *Engaging Children's Minds: The Project Approach.* Norwood, N.J.: Ablex, 1989.

8. Peterson, K. *Building Curriculum for Young Children: Deciding on*

Content. ED 297886, 1988.

9. Robison, H., and Spodek, B. *New Directions in the Kindergarten.* New York: Teachers College Press, 1965.

10. Spodek, B. *Teaching in the Early Years.* 3d ed. Englewood Cliffs, N.J.: Prentice Hall, 1985.

11. ____. "Conceptualizing Today's Kindergarten Curriculum." *Elementary School Journal* 89, no. 2 (1988): 203–11.

12. Spodek, B.; Saracho, O. N.; and Davis, M. D. *Foundations of Early Childhood Education.* 2d ed. Englewood Cliffs, N.J.: Prentice Hall, 1991.

APPENDIX:
INTEGRATING THE TOPIC
INTO THE CURRICULUM

Possible Field Trips

> Restaurant
> Grocery Store
> Farm, Orchard
> Factory (where food is processed)
> Bakery
> Farmers' Market

Stories

An Apple Is Red, by Nancy Curry. Glendale, Calif.: Bowmar, 1967.

Blueberries for Sal, by Robert McCloskey. New York: Viking Press, 1948.

Bread and Jam for Frances, by Russell Hoban. New York: Harper and Row, 1964.

The Carrot Seed, by Ruth Krauss. New York: Harper and Row, 1945.

The Gingerbread Boy, by Paul Goldone. New York, Clarion Books, 1979. (Note: Many versions of this story are available.)

Journey Cake Ho, by Ruth Sawyer. New York: Viking Press, 1978.

Little Red Hen, by Paul Goldone. New York: Clarion Books, 1985. (Note: Many versions of this story are available.)

Potato Pancakes All Around, by Marilyn Hirsch. Philadelphia: Jewish Publication Society of America, 1982.

Stone Soup, by Marcia Brown. New York: Macmillan, 1986.

Strega Nona, by Tomie dePaola. Englewood Cliffs, N.J.: Prentice Hall, 1975.

The Very Hungry Caterpillar, by Eric Carle. Cleveland: Collins-World, 1970.

Songs

"Aikendrum," "Cluck, Cluck, Red Hen," "The Corner Grocery Store," and "The Fruitbasket Song." *Raffi Singable Songbook.* Don Mills, Ont., Canada: Chappell. (Also available on record)

"Did You Feed My Cow?" (Available on record) *American Negro Folk and Worksong Rhythms.* Scholastic, SC7654.

"Do You Know the Muffin Man?" and "Oats, Peas, Beans, and Barley Grow." *Songs for Early Childhood.* Louisville, Ky.: Westminster Press.

"Old MacDonald Had a Farm." *Old MacDonald Had a Farm,* by Robert Quackenbush. Philadelphia: Lippincott, 1972.

"Pease Porridge Hot," "The Farmer in the Dell," and "Hot Cross Buns." *Complete Nursery Songbook,* by Inez Bertail. New York: Lothrop, Lee and Shepard, 1947.

"What Do You Do on the Farm?" *American Folk Songs for Children.* New York: Doubleday and Co.

Dramatic Play Activities

(Opportunities for language, literacy, mathematics, and social learning)

Set up a grocery store next to the housekeeping area:
- Collect empty food boxes, cans, etc.
- Provide cash register and play money.

- Provide aprons for grocer.
- Include shopping carts or baskets, and bags.
- Provide paper, pencils or crayons, and tape so that children can put prices on grocery items and make grocery lists.
- Include coupons for shoppers.
- Provide a food scale for weighing.

In housekeeping area:

- Be sure to have pots and pans for cooking.
- Use pretend food or have children "make" food by pasting magazine pictures of food on paper plates or using playdough.
- Include empty food containers.
- Provide paper and pencils or crayons for children who want to make shopping lists before going to the store.

Other Activities to Promote Literacy Learning

- Make books about field trip.
- Draw class mural of field trip with story included.
- Write recipes for cooking activities.
- Record what happens in cooking activities, such as making butter, peanut butter, applesauce, etc.

Other Activities in Math and Science

- Make bar graph of what children eat for breakfast or lunch, or of favorite foods in the classroom; children could paste equally sized squares of colored paper to a tagboard chart, or they could make a three dimensional bar graph with small blocks.
- Provide children with different types of scales to weigh classroom objects.
- Make charts of children's heights and weights.
- Grow plants from seeds; observe how they grow under

different conditions, chart their growth.

- Cooking Activities: Allow children to measure ingredients, count number of cups or teaspoonfuls added; show how one food can be eaten many different ways, and how different processes change the shape, texture, and color of food (for example: an apple can be eaten raw, dried, cooked into applesauce, baked in a pie, or drunk as juice; also butter, peanut butter, popcorn).

Art Activities and Activities That Provide for a Variety of Learning (playdough, sand, water, blocks)

(In some classrooms teachers may not feel comfortable using food for anything other than eating; each teacher will need to make this decision.)

- Have children cut out magazine pictures of food for a collage or to paste on paper plates for use in the housekeeping area.
- Use fruits and vegetables to make prints.
- Color pasta with food coloring for stringing as beads.
- Make collages with pasta and dried beans.
- Put rice (instead of sand) in sand table for pouring, measuring, touching.
- Provide cooking utensils—pots, cookie cutters, spatulas— with playdough.
- Provide plastic or wooden animals for block area; children can make a barn out of a box.
- Provide "still life" near easel for children to paint.

Movement Activities

- Listen to "Sammy"—a song about a child who hops, flies, swims, and crawls to the store to buy bread (*Getting to Know Myself,* record by Hap Palmer, Activity Records, AR543); children can make up other ways to go to the store.

39

- Do exercises to help build healthy, strong bodies.
- Use some of the songs mentioned earlier for movement activities.

3. LONG-TERM PROJECTS

by Melanie Turnipseed Kenney

Most early childhood education programs organize activities into relatively simple, short units of time. This organization often reflects a concern for young children's short attention span and interest. However, there is a place for long-term extended projects in the early childhood classroom as well. Long-term projects provide a natural learning environment in which the cognitive, social, and motor development of young children is allowed to emerge as they explore topics at their own developmental level. This chapter will discuss how teachers might create a classroom atmosphere to nurture the emergence, the development, and the expansion of long-term extended projects. It will also discuss how to evaluate and end a long-term extended project, and provide examples to clarify what is meant by long-term extended projects.

The environment in which long-term projects are supported is one in which cooperation, exploration, child-directedness, flexibility, and creativity are valued. Johnson and Johnson (1) define the cooperative classroom as one that fosters positive interdependence, face-to-face interaction, individual accountability, and interpersonal skills in a natural setting. This noncompetitive setting avoids didactic instruction, and nurtures interaction between participants. Furthermore, long-term projects in a cooperative setting promote self- and peer-regulation, the exchange of ideas, and a continued motivation to learn (1). In such an atmosphere children learn to negotiate difficulties, practice their social skills, and develop problem solving strategies. Long-term projects offer the opportunity for children at all ability levels to learn to care for one another, and to function as individuals within a group—skills that are so important to maturing individuals in families, in communities, and on the job.

Play is the key element in long-term projects. Play is intrinsically motivated and is relatively free of externally imposed rules; it extends through the child's world, requires the active involvement of the players, and is dominated by the players rather than by adults (2). This play provides the pathway for the development of a long-term project, as seen in the example of the building of a mass transit district bus in the classroom. The conceptualization, implementation, and daily reflection on the project allowed guided educational play to enhance cognitive, social, emotional, and motor development for all the children involved.

THE MTD BUS: A LONG-TERM PROJECT

The first step in planning a long-term project is to identify a familiar and/or particular interest of the children. Picking up on children's interests as a basis for school activities motivates them to further their understanding of the world. In the case of the mass transit district (MTD) bus project described here, most children in our community have ridden on the bus and are familiar with this means of transportation. A field trip was arranged to the mass transit district bus garage and headquarters. This field trip introduced a few of the children to the MTD bus. It also helped the other children focus on and experience more deeply a mode of transportation already familiar to them.

The field trip was instigated by a child talking about riding the bus to the shopping mall with his mother. The teacher captured that teachable moment and encouraged the child to expand his thoughts while she included other children in the discussion about local bus travel. The field trip was arranged and confirmed after the teacher and the manager of the mass transit district discussed what might be of interest to these young children. The field trip encouraged children to spontaneously expound and exclaim interest in such things as buses, tools, and accessories that they saw during this time. The teacher took many photographs of the children observing and investigating various objects and buses during the field trip. These photographs were instrumental in the development of the MTD bus project. At the end of the field trip, the class rode the MTD bus around town. The field trip stimulated many activities yet to be discovered.

Creating Supportive Conditions

In order to gain maximum benefit from the field trip, the teacher looked for ways to recapture the experience. The children later reviewed and discussed in class the photos taken on the trip. Collective writing activities with small groups of children and the class as a whole served this purpose. Having the teacher write the children's dictated thoughts and feelings about the field trip promoted language growth and nurtured cooperation in the classroom. As a group effort, this writing also discouraged competition and limited the isolation of individual children.

In the days that followed, the teacher's conversations encouraged children to recreate their experience and project how it might be followed up in the classroom. The children were asked what might be needed to build a bus. "What do we need to do first?" "How can we do that?" The teacher served as a facilitator and also recorded the ideas emerging from the children's creative minds.

The bus project did not begin with ready-made materials or with a preconceived notion of what should happen. Rather, it began with an interest, a teachable moment, a field trip, and extensions of the children's experience. The children and the community were the resources. Self-confidence and knowledge of the world were not the only dimensions being developed in the project; oral and written language were developed as well. The teacher and children began discussing and recording their experience early. The teacher encouraged using language and recall as they wrote captions and stories about the field-trip photographs. Details of the experience were highlighted and the children delighted in reliving the experience. Lists and stories were instantaneously recorded from group discussions. The project already seemed important to the children. Thus, meaningful language and communication and greater understanding emerged from their involvement with the project.

Implementing the Project

Involvement was about to be extended since interest and enthusiasm indicated that it was time to engage the children in new related activities. The teacher and children jointly planned to build an MTD bus. The teacher provided the lumber, nails, saws, work table, safety glasses, and a variety of other necessary things. She also created a safe physical environment that allowed production of the bus to proceed. Because the children were not capable of conceiving of the entire plan for constructing a bus, the teacher took the leadership in the project and laid out the frame. The children, however, did the actual work of sawing the wood and nailing the pieces they had cut together to create the frame, with the teacher intervening only for reasons of safety. The children themselves decided when someone else would hammer or saw as they got tired or were ready to move on to a different activity. The teacher showed how to use tools properly and safely. She also extended children's conversations about the bus through the building process. Throughout this building stage, there was a continuing dialogue among the children, between children and adults, and, sometimes, between children and materials. The building process was slow, but rewarding because children could see the progress made each day. Language, cognitive, motor, and social skills of each participant were continuously being extended within a spirit of cooperation. The daily work on the project was enhanced by regular reflection and projection of the project itself. Individually or as a group, children were encouraged to recognize what had been done, what needed to be done, and what materials were needed each day as they reviewed the day's activities. Construction of the wooden frame took about two to three weeks. Adding the cardboard exterior and painting it took about the same amount of time. Creating and adding accessories, including seats, steering wheel, heater, seat belts, mirrors, windshield wipers, and lights took another few weeks. The entire project lasted more than three months.

Extending the Project

The children initiated and created the bus accessories. Some of the interests and details were a direct result of discussions held during the daily reflection time, while others were extrapolated from the photographs taken on the field trip and from their captions. Once again the teacher provided a variety of materials for the children. The headlights were made from coffee filters, the windshield wipers from pipe cleaners, the seat belts were created from strips of fabric, and the mirrors from aluminum foil. As the children began to use the bus for "real trips," they realized that money and a money box were also needed. Continued play and interaction between classmates spawned the need for even more accessories, such as street signs and advertisements, which in turn supported extended play. The details were endless and were always the direct result of ideas that children shared. In addition, the teacher followed the leads of the children, helping them to understand their experiences. The teacher continually served as a resource and provider of needed materials—items that were open-ended and that invited children to be creative. The unrestricted nature of the materials motivated the children and supported the cooperative nature of the MTD bus project.

The children took many magnificent imaginary trips on the bus. They went to stores and fast-food restaurants, the zoo, and grandma's, to name just a few places. Even more interesting than the destinations were the dialogues that took place during the travel. The teacher heard conversations about a variety of topics: seat belts, what children did before getting on the bus, why the bus was late, bus breakdowns, repair work, how long it would take to get somewhere, and what to do if the bus was full. The rich language reflected the children's interactions with each other, their experiences, and the project as a whole.

BENEFITS OF LONG-TERM PROJECTS

Working on a long-term project, such as the mass transit district bus, exemplifies what can result from a field trip. A long-term project is a medium that young children plan, implement, and make progress in, using new-found problem-solving strategies. For example, children learned how to deal with such problems as whether the construction was sturdy enough and how to attach the colored cellophane for the bus windows. Together they discussed and solved these problems. They fastened the colored windows by having one child tear the tape and another hand the tape out as needed while two other children held the colored cellophane. A group of children were perplexed about getting tires for the bus. They decided to ask other teachers in the school for tires. Not only was this a strategy that might solve their problem, but it also provided an opportunity for a small group of children to practice the social graces of entering another classroom and asking a question. Incidentally, tires were found in the janitor's room. There were enough to place three tires on one side and two on the other.

A complex, long-term extended project such as this one allows children to engage in different activities of varying degrees of difficulty so that each child can function adequately at his or her level. The project can thus accommodate the individual differences to be found among the children in the class. Not all kindergartners are developmentally ready for higher-level interactions. The long-term project provides learning opportunities for the child who engages in solitary play as well. A child might work on a specific activity such as painting the bus, reinforcing the junction of two 2 x 4's—work that might not require interaction with others. Because a long-term project can accommodate all children at various stages of development, no child needs to be left out. The completed bus was not the only product of the group effort. Children developed planning skills, they learned to use tools, they did research, engaged in discussions, and planned activities to carry out the decisions they made. The affective domain was developed as well. Students who worked together on this project developed considerable commitment and caring for each other as well for the project; a sense of pride emerged.

Another important aspect of the long-term project was the period of time it took to finish. In a world where we tend to seek instant gratification, a long-term project provides extended realistic daily pursuits of a long-term goal while at the same time yielding measurable success along the way. In the case of the MTD bus, construction of the eight- by ten-foot bus began in January and ended in late March. The extensive process was as important to the children as the product.

The continuing nature and development of a long-term project is a result of the children's minds and the environment interacting with and challenging each other. Children grow from the challenges that result from their own direct action on the environment. They learn to resolve conflicts that can naturally occur. The resolution of such conflicts is something they need to learn. For example, using tools, taking turns, and being in the way of another child were common situational conflicts that occurred with the MTD bus project. Children were encouraged to practice their social skills and deal with these conflicts themselves. The teacher let the children discover their own strategies for dealing with the conflicts that arose, although sometimes the teacher did interject positive social statements to encourage negotiations.

Uninterrupted time was a very important part of the learning process described here. Children need large blocks of time both on a daily and weekly basis to develop and carry through their ideas without interruption (2). The absence of interruptions and the extension of the project for weeks and months also helped the children expand their thoughts, their caring, and their contributions to a group effort.

EVALUATION

How does one evaluate the worth of something that took weeks to create and to extend, or the accomplishment of each child who was involved? Certainly not with a worksheet or a standardized test. Teachers need to observe the children in their activities and seek indicators of their learning and growth in the project. They need to collect samples of the children's work and their language, analyzing each product within its context to judge the learning that has taken place. The learning process itself also needs to be studied and evaluated. Some questions to guide the teacher's observations and assessments follow.

What indicators are there of the children's language development? Are they using new vocabulary? Is their speech more descriptive? Are their utterances more complex? Are they more responsive to one another in conversations?

Has the children's play changed? Are they more social in their play? Are they able to elaborate play ideas and extend them into other areas? Are they using play materials more imaginatively?

Are the children cooperating more with each other? Are they developing better social skills? Did they resolve problems that resulted from the use of tools and the demand for materials? Are they building lasting friendships?

Are the children involved mentally and physically with their activities? Are they planning activities and carrying out their plans? Are they able to see relationships between the things they observed on field trips and what occurs in the classroom?

These are just a few of the questions that need to be asked for a proper evaluation. The teacher needs to examine whether the children explored spatial, qualitative, and quantitative concepts through their play. Evaluation should be a continuing process that permeates the teacher's daily reflections on the thoughts and actions of the children. It is also helpful if the teacher jots down notes that illustrate how individuals understand and apply new concepts. Just as the curriculum is not prepackaged, so too evaluation should not be prepackaged.

SUMMARY

The mass transit bus project can be summarized in the following sequence. The project began with an interest of the children, followed by a field trip, planning, building, planning/reflecting, playing, and adding accessories as needed—all leading to extended play. The project lasted for three months. It was not until the children's interest seemed to waiver that ending the project was considered. When children no longer voluntarily played or discussed the MTD bus, then it was time to change the classroom focus.

Several features contribute to the success of such long-term projects as the one described here. One of the features is a cooperative setting with limited time restraints that allow children to discover knowledge through their own manipulation and direct involvement with the setting, people, and materials. The integrative spirit that develops in such a project cannot be enhanced by didactic instruction that attempts to have children conform to a prescribed curriculum. A cooperative environment does not automatically occur. Teachers must convey a message of shared responsibility with children, thinking of themselves as resource persons and facilitators rather than as instructors; they must be active participants in the process. Time must be allocated for reflection and representation to enhance the children's understanding of their own world and experiences. Teachers also need to share their authority with children and allow them to solve conflicts and problem situations. Long-term projects optimally develop when the environment and the teacher both favor shared growth and the creation of meaningful experiences.

The importance of the process rather than the product has been stressed throughout this chapter. This process of development is not only necessary for the project itself, but is also most important for the young child. When children are engaged in a meaningful long-term extended project, they have many continuing opportunities to learn. They can explore the process of language growth, cognitive development, motor development, social skills, and their own affect. As a result of interacting with their peers and the environment, they process new information. Long-term projects optimally provide children with opportunities to assimilate new knowledge and accommodate their previously learned knowledge to the new understandings that arise within their own developmental levels.

Educators recognize that children are a wonderful resource; this was true for those who built and played in the bus. For example, one child's mother had just begun to work in a local hospital. The child visited the hospital and, returning to school, shared this experience with others in the classroom. The bus that the children had built was transformed into a hospital through their ingenuity and creativity. And so the story continues.

The key element in the development of a long-term extended project is the play that comes naturally for the young child. A long-term project accommodates, encourages, and expands play at each child's developmental level and comfort zone. It is this play that allowed the MTD bus to be built, played in, written about, and used for wonderful imaginative trips. It is this natural play that nurtures cognitive growth within the child. A long-term project is more than something to do in the classroom to keep children busy. It is a vehicle that permits play and learning to be integrated and balanced within all aspects of the children's functioning.

REFERENCES

1. Johnson, D. W., and Johnson, R. T. *Circles of Learning.* Alexandria, Va.: Association for Supervision and Curriculum Development, 1984.

2. Rogers, C. S., and Sawyers, J. K. *Play in the Lives of Children.* Washington, D.C.: National Association for the Education of Young Children, 1988.

3. Rowland, S. *The Enquiring Classroom.* Basingstoke, England: Taylor and Francis, 1987.

4. Spodek, B., ed. *Today's Kindergarten: Exploring the Knowledge Base, Expanding the Curriculum.* New York: Teachers College Press, 1986.

ADDITIONAL RESOURCES

Bruner, J. *Under Fives in Britain.* London: High/Scope Press, 1980.

Croft, D. J., and Hess, R. D. *An Activities Handbook for Teachers of Young Children.* Boston: Houghton, Mifflin, 1975.

Herr, J., and Libby, Y. *Designing Creative Materials for Young Children.* New York: Harcourt Brace Jovanovich, 1990.

Palmer, R. *Space, Time and Grouping.* New York: Citation Press, 1971.

Raines, S. C., and Canady, R. *Story Stretchers.* Mt. Rainier, Md.: Gryphon House, 1989.

Rance, P. *Teaching by Topics.* London: Redwood Press, 1968.

Trostle, S. L., and Yawkey, T. D. *Integrated Learning Activities for Young Children.* Boston: Allyn and Bacon, 1990.

Warren, J. *Theme-a-saurus.* Everett, Wash.: Warren Publishing House, 1989.

Wilmes, D., and Wilmes, L. *Yearful of Circle Time.* Elgin, Ill.: Building Blocks, 1989.

4. FOSTERING EMERGENT LITERACY IN A PUBLISHING CENTER

by Jeanette Allison Hartman

Within the past two decades views of the reading process have changed as the field of reading and language arts has been reconceptualized as "language and literacy." Research shows that successful readers not only have a repertoire of reading strategies, but also use comprehension strategies contributing to communicative competency. They understand and apply their knowledge and skills to writing, speaking, and listening as well as to reading (1, 8, 9). It is these understandings and the ability to apply them that have become the basis for educating young children in language and literacy.

Studies on children's emerging literacy also show that language experiences need to include both spontaneous and deliberate activities that include all functions of communication: reading, writing, listening, and speaking. Including a full range of communication skills that reflects an interactive model of literacy emphasizes the interaction between the learner and both oral and written language (3, 5).

Projects can offer children relevant experiences with both oral and written language. As presented here, a publishing center project can offer children intellectually rich experiences that foster their emerging literacy by using natural interactions and common everyday artifacts. Such a publishing center project is appropriate for the kindergarten. Because the center represents a rather complex, long-term project, it might best be started well into the kindergarten year. By that time the children will have developed a sense of the kindergarten's organization and will be able to function more independently. The teacher will have helped the children develop a sense of reading and writing and of the relationship of oral to written language, as well as some literacy skills.

The publishing center project is educationally worthwhile, meeting Spodek's criteria (7) for selecting educationally appropriate topics. It integrates the concepts learned rather than presenting them in isolation. These concepts are readily related to the children's existing knowledge base. The materials used are accessible and relate to the children's daily lives. In addition, the activities are balanced and provide a whole literacy perspective.

GOALS FOR A PUBLISHING CENTER PROJECT

The goals of this project help children comprehend publishing as well as develop literacy skills. Among the concepts children should develop are the following:

a. Publishing helps communication and transmits ideas.

b. There are many specific roles in publishing.

c. Publishing produces various useful literary materials (e.g., books, stationery, posters).

d. Books and other written materials are the products of publishing.

e. Many people work in publishing occupations.

f. Many materials are used in publishing (e.g., paper, ink).

Not all children will attain these concepts to the same degree, but each child should have some understanding of them. The children will gain other concepts as well. Understanding publishing requires many different skills and concepts from content areas such as social studies, mathematics, language arts, science, and art.

PLANNING AND PREPARING FOR THE PROJECT

The publishing center project can evolve through three phases. The first phase might include group meetings and a field trip. During group meetings children can discuss the purposes and products of a publishing center. The teacher could ask: "What do you think a publishing center is? What happens at a publishing center? How could we use a publishing center?" The children's comments could be recorded on a large piece of paper for all to see. Materials related to a publishing center could be passed around and discussed.

Children can take a field trip to observe publishing activities in a newspaper office, a publisher's office, or a print shop during this phase. Field trips stimulate interest and provide children with new and fresh ideas. If such a trip is not feasible, invite a newspaper employee, editor, artist, illustrator, author, or printer to your class.

Neighborhood walks can also stimulate interest in printed material. Such a walk could provide opportunities to observe and talk about print in the environment (e.g., billboards, flyers on telephone poles). The children can also be helped to observe the relationship between printed words and other symbols, such as pictures, logos, and the like. During the walk a local newspaper could be purchased.

FOLLOWUP ACTIVITIES
AND CONSTRUCTING THE CENTER

The second phase of the project includes followup activities from the field trip and constructing a center in the classroom. At this time, children, parents, and teachers bring in materials necessary for constructing a publishing center. Children could draw their idea of the publishing center's physical structure and also use tape to map out a plan for the space to be used on the floor. Prepare the classroom for the project, allocating space and providing basic materials as needed: large and medium-sized cardboard boxes and soft pine wood scraps for construction, measuring instruments, tools and nails, tape and glue, markers and chalk, paint and brushes, various sizes of styrofoam, and floor covering (old shower curtains work well). If available, blocks should be provided. These could be unit blocks, large plastic connecting blocks, or larger wooden hollow blocks. Materials for homemade books, signs, and posters also should be provided. The children can construct these from scratch.

Next, you could begin constructing the publishing center. The children could make a frame of cardboard or wood, or use the existing language arts area of the room as the publishing center. Throughout this phase, group meetings could be held to talk about the project. Such meetings provide children continuous opportunities to plan, as well as to reflect on their activity and to help the teacher evaluate the project's progress.

In constructing a publishing center, it would be helpful to have materials that represent a publishing center or a local newspaper business. Children will also need to talk about the people in a publishing business in order to support their role-playing efforts.

Role playing (i.e., sociodramatic play) is a major vehicle for children's learning. Although role playing is often thought of as a child-initiated activity, it can be goal-directed. You will need to collect props to entice children's curiosities and to support their activities, providing opportunities to use their knowledge in extended activity. Individual roles will also need to be identified. Publishing roles and related materials include:

Authors: blank books, paper, writing instruments, computer, and typewriter

Illustrators: pens, pencils, markers, colored pencils, chalk, paint, sketching paper, easel, and art paper

Printer: empty, clean ink containers; ink pads and stamps, paper, and glue

Binders: paper; products from editors, printers, and illustrators; glue, a child-constructed "binding" machine, and packaging materials

Sales Clerks: cash register, assorted real money (coins), telephone, order forms, old checks, receipt pads, and typewriter

Consumers: bookstore buyers, stationery supply buyers, students, teachers

In planning for the publishing center activities, teachers need to decide what materials and equipment will be needed and how time and space will be organized in the classroom. They also should consider the human resources needed. Resource persons who know about various aspects of the publishing enterprise can be invited to talk to and work with the children. Parents or retirees may be invited into the classroom to help work with small groups of children on various aspects of the project. Children from the upper grades can also act as resources.

Kindergarten children differ from one another in a variety of ways. The differences in language abilities will certainly become evident in such a project. Some children will have attained a high level of language skills, possibly even reading and writing before they enter kindergarten. Other children will still have a long way to go in the development of their literacy skills. A variety of tasks can be planned in the publishing center to reflect the variety of competencies in the classroom.

Although there are many possible publishing center activities, this chapter presents four activities related to the construction of a publishing center: (a) constructing a publishing center, (b) the finished structure, (c) the functioning structure, and (d) writing, illustrating, and producing a book. Curriculum webs (4) are included for each activity.

ACTIVITY 1: CONSTRUCTING A PUBLISHING CENTER (WEB #1)

Rationale

Children learn about social concepts best by actively exploring roles. Constructing a publishing center allows children to help create the setting for their later activities and, through that creation, understand the entire process.

Objectives

- The children will plan and construct a publishing center, participating in various construction roles.

- The children will learn about new and familiar roles and elements of construction (e.g., electrician, construction worker, foundation, walls, wood, and cardboard).

- The children will learn that materials scavenged from home and school can be put to good use in school.

Integrated Learnings

Social Studies: Many different people contribute to building a publishing center; every role is important; if one part is missing, then the whole suffers.

Language Arts: Symbolic activities, such as drawing up plans, making blueprints, and developing lists, are useful in planning and organizing a project. New vocabulary is learned related to new activity areas.

Math: Measuring is needed to plan a construction. Parts need to be adapted (cut, added to) and shaped to fit together. The children will also classify similar and different roles and materials, seriating and ordering steps in construction, weighing materials, and graphing their progress.

Science: The children can later test predictions made during planning and observe change. They can develop and test hypotheses, such as: How much wood or cardboard will it take to build the frame? How many nails or how much glue will be needed to secure the frame? Would nails or glue be more secure with wood, with cardboard?

Physical Education: The children will learn to use different muscles during construction. They can talk about how the heart works harder while moving around, hammering, carrying wood, and sawing than when writing or typing.

Materials

These materials will be needed: books, pictures, posters, various sizes of pine wood (safe, easy to work with), refrigerator and dishwasher boxes, miscellaneous boxes, hammers, screwdrivers, saws, woodworking tables, nails, screws, measuring tape, rulers, glue, duct tape, rope, string, vices, clamps, hard hats, shower curtains or newspapers for floor covering, tempera paint, paintbrushes, markers, aprons, large paper for blueprints, and poster board.

Procedures

Before the beginning of Activity 1, the children would have visited a publishing, printing, or newspaper business. Upon returning to the classroom, they could discuss and draw the publishing center, including products, occupations, and materials.

Parents can be asked to help collect the necessary materials. The children could make blueprints or drawings of the evolving center. After blueprints are made, they could begin construction with wood or cardboard. If wood is used, children will need help with the whole frame construction. A parent aide or volunteer could be a useful resource here. If a refrigerator or washer box is used, the children will need help to outline windows, doors, entrances, and exits. After the frame is built, the teacher should help the children as they do the actual

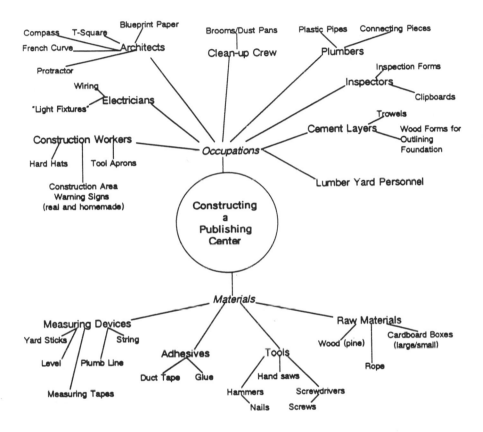

construction. The teacher should also talk with the children about their activities and record their ideas, charting their progress daily.

ACTIVITY 2: THE FINISHED STRUCTURE (WEB #2)

Rationale

Children will benefit from continuous learning experiences. By allowing them to continue constructing the publishing center, they will participate in related activities over a long period of time. The finished structure will enable them to focus on details of the center before they enter into Activity 3.

Objectives

- Children should make decisions about aspects of the publishing center features such as color, location of doors and "light fixtures," and other elements. (The teacher needs to provide guidance.)

Integrated Learnings

Social Studies: Many different people contribute to a building; every role is important.

Language Arts: Labels help individuals identify things and places as well as their use. Posters can tell people about products.

Math: Classification, seriation, and ordering will continue; weighing materials; graphing progress.

Science: Children will observe change over extended periods of time. They will continue to predict and experiment with materials, observing change, validating or modifying hypotheses.

Art: Painting and design work can make the publishing center attractive.

Materials

These materials will be needed: tempera paint, markers, wallpaper scraps, glue, string, paintbrushes, carpet scraps, yarn or safe wiring, styrofoam, mailboxes, paper, envelopes, and "postage," desks, chairs, ink pads and stamps, poster board, fabric, small boxes, office supply items, and labels (construction paper, sticky labels).

Procedures

Activity 1 will probably extend into Activity 2. The goal here is to finish the construction and designate areas according to function. Finishing touches include painting, wallpapering, carpeting, labeling, and advertising. Continue with talking and writing about children's progress.

Wallpapering Tools

Wallpaper Scraps

Flyers   Posters   Paint Supplies   Aprons

Advertisers   Wallpaperers   Painters

Inspection Forms

Inspectors

Wiring   Clipboards

"Light Fixtures"   Electricians

Carpet Layers

Dry Wall People   Occupations   Carpet Scraps

Dry Wall
Tools

Publishing Center Owners

Finished Structure

Materials

Measuring Devices   Raw Materials

Yard Sticks   String   Glue   Wallpaper   Carpet Scraps

Adhesives   Brushes   Scraps

Level   Plumb Line   Tools   Fixtures/

Features   Tempera Paint

Duct Tape   Glue

Measuring Tapes   Hammers   Screwdrivers   Light   Phones   Paint Brushes

Nails   Screws   Fixtures   Sponges

Sandpaper

(Large styrofoam pieces work well)

ACTIVITY 3: A FUNCTIONING PUBLISHING CENTER (WEB #3)

Rationale

Children are curious about print and language. Experimenting with different roles and functions provides them with oral and written language experiences. The functioning structure provides them with a natural extension of previous learning experiences.

Objectives

- The children will establish a functioning publishing center.
- The children will experiment with and talk about different publishing center materials.
- The children will begin to construct homemade books.
- The children will continue to experiment with oral and written language, expressing their ideas in illustrative forms.

Integrated Learnings

Language Arts: Language can be expressed in many different forms. Oral language can be transposed into written language. Writing involves thinking about ideas, writing them down, editing, revising, and sharing what is written. There are different genres of literature such as realism, folk tales, and fantasy.

Social Studies: Many different people contribute their efforts and talents to a publishing center. Books can express the ideas and feelings that many people share.

Art: Published products require many different forms of art. Ideas expressed as illustrations enhance the text. Illustrations, photographs, and paintings alone can tell a story.

Math: Making a book involves estimating the number of

pages needed and measuring the book cover dimensions. Literature needs to be sorted by genres, such as fiction and nonfiction.

Science: There are different properties of art media and publishing materials such as ink and glue.

Materials

Continue using the materials from Activity 2. Additional materials will be needed for homemade books (e.g., tagboard, paper, writing and coloring tools, glue and yarn).

Procedures

You may want to invite a publishing center guest to help the children. Have them designate areas for different activities. Where will the authors write? They can also assign themselves different roles. Who will bind our books? Should we have a cashier? Help the children set up materials according to the designated areas. Have children select their roles. Roles can change within the session or each day.

Web #3

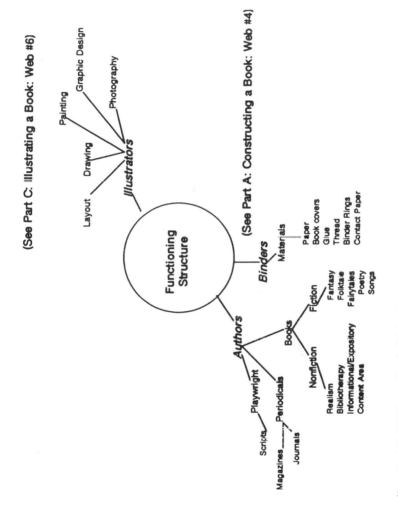

(See Part C: Illustrating a Book: Web #6)

Illustrators
- Layout
- Drawing
- Painting
- Graphic Design
- Photography

Functioning Structure

(See Part A: Constructing a Book: Web #4)

Binders
- Materials
  - Paper
  - Book covers
  - Glue
  - Thread
  - Binder Rings
  - Contact Paper

Authors
- Playwright
  - Scripts
- Periodicals
  - Magazines
  - Journals
- Books
  - Fiction
    - Fantasy
    - Folktale
    - Fairytales
    - Poetry
    - Songs
  - Nonfiction
    - Realism
    - Bibliotherapy
    - Informational/Expository
    - Content Area

(See Part B: Writing a Book: Web #5)

ACTIVITY 4: WRITING, ILLUSTRATING, AND PRODUCING A BOOK (WEBS #4–6)

Rationale

Children enjoy making artifacts and projects reflecting the ideas they learn at school. They will translate their oral, expressive language into written language and participate in all aspects of book construction, including illustration.

Objectives

- The children will learn the purposes and genres of books.

- The children will learn about the different people who create books.
- The children will learn what materials are needed to make books.

Part A: Producing a Book (Web #4)

Materials

These materials will be needed: various qualities of paper, tag- or cardboard, glue, thread, large sewing needles, binder rings, paper punchers, scissors, contact paper, and rulers.

Procedures

Have the children decide what size book they want (e.g., dimensions, number of pages). Be sure they have enough pages but are still able to sew them together; they could use binder rings instead of thread. If they use contact paper for a cover, have them measure the correct amount and help them put it on the cover. As the children work, help them use the new vocabulary in their discussions (e.g., binding, spine of the book, contact paper, blank pages, binder, author, illustrator). Focus on how their ideas and words will become print.

Part B: Writing a Book (Web #5)

Materials

These materials will be needed: homemade books from Part A, large and small pencils, erasers, and computer(s), paper, and glue (computer paper can be glued onto book pages).

Procedures

Encourage the children to interact and collaborate with each other. Talk about: (1) the purpose of the book (e.g., informational, recreational, narrative); (2) the book's length; (3) the writing process (e.g., editing, revising, sharing); and (4) the genre of the book (e.g., autobiography, realism, fantasy). Have the children provide a title, author's name, illustrator's name, and table of contents (if any) for their book. Encourage them to share their experiences in writing/authoring a book. Provide an author's corner.

Part C: Illustrating a Book (Web #6)

Materials

These materials will be needed: for drawing—ink, chalk, colored pencils, charcoal, crayons; for painting—watercolors, grease pencils, tempera, stencils, oil paint; for posters—poster board, tagboard, large markers, drawing and painting supplies; for graphic design—computers, various mediums such as magazines, pictures, sketches; for photography—camera (primary source), magazines, flyers, old books, photocopies (secondary source), and so forth.

Procedures

Brainstorm with the children as to possible illustrations

that "fit" each homemade book. Discuss what materials would be best and how different materials have different effects. Graph children's responses. For example, ask them how they feel when viewing black and white charcoal illustrations as in Wanda Gag's *Millions of Cats* compared to Leo Lionni's *Swimmy* illustrated in pastel colors.

Web #4:
Part A: Constructing a Book

Web #5:
Part B: Writing a Book

Web #6:
Part C: Illustrating a Book

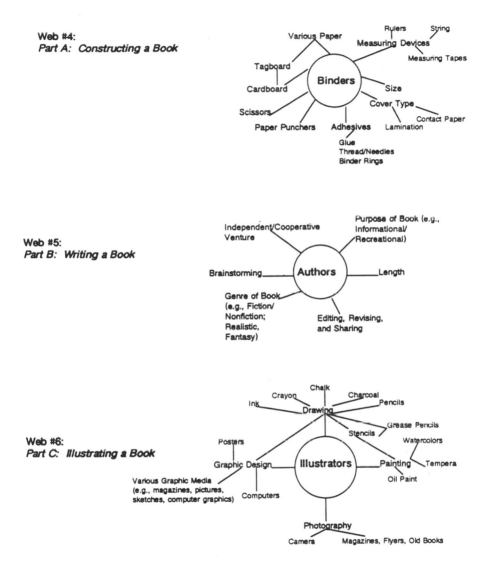

EVALUATING THE PUBLISHING CENTER PROJECT

The third phase of the project includes evaluating the publishing center. You can use an informal assessment or a more formal assessment for this project as well as for its separate parts. Informal assessment is often more appropriate at the kindergarten level.

Teachers will want to evaluate the activities themselves, to determine if they did accomplish what was intended. In addition, the outcomes resulting from the activities should be assessed. Teachers can collect information on children's learning during the project using a variety of informal assessments, including anecdotal records, checklists, interviews, and samples of children's work. This material can be gathered into portfolios and kept over extended periods of time (2, 6).

A number of questions can be asked to guide the evaluation. In regard to the activities:

- How much did children do on their own and with each other?

- Did children follow through with activities?

- Were children eager to participate in various roles?

- Did children understand the uses of oral and written language?

- Did children approach errors as learning opportunities?

- Did children participate in charting, graphing, writing, editing, reading, and sharing their ideas?

- Did children make predictions and revise and validate their predictions?

- Did children label publishing center features?

- Were children involved in the whole process: idea

starting, planning, gathering, and working with materials?

- Were children interested in talking with each other about the publishing center?

- Did children remember the publishing center or local newspaper field trip(s)?

- Were materials accessible to children and related to their daily lives?

- Did children participate in both informal and formal as well as short- and long-term learning?

- Were the concepts that were taught integrated across content areas as much as possible?

In regard to learning outcomes:

- Was growth evident in children's use of language?

- Did children demonstrate comprehension of new vocabulary with familiar vocabulary?

- Did children increase their use of written language during the activities?

- Did children's language skills improve?

- Were understandings in other learning areas (e.g., math, social studies, art) more evident after the activities?

SUGGESTED PUBLISHING CENTER ADAPTATIONS

This project, like most projects, can have a finite life, or it can be extended into a variety of related areas. Among the related areas that can be used as a basis for project adaptation are the following:

71

- a local newspaper business
- a "Writing Workshop" (see Resources section for video)
- a stationery shop
- a message center
- a post office
- a library.

REFERENCES

1. Anderson, R. C.; Hiebert, E. H.; Scott, J. A.; and Wilkinson, I. A. G. *Becoming a Nation of Readers: The Report of the Commission on Reading.* Washington, D.C.: National Institute of Education, 1985.

2. Canbourne, B., and Turbill, J. "Assessment in Whole Language Classrooms." *Elementary School Journal* 90 (1990): 337–49.

3. Clay, M. *Reading: The Patterning of Complex Behavior.* 2d ed. Auckland, N.Z.: Heinemann Educational Books, 1979.

4. Corwin, C.; Hein, G. E.; and Levin, D. "Weaving Curriculum Webs: The Structure of Nonlinear Curriculum." *Childhood Education* 52, no. 5 (1976): 248–51.

5. Mason, J. M. "A Problem-Solving Approach to Reading." In *Today's Kindergarten,* edited by B. Spodek, 48–66. New York: Teachers College Press, 1986.

6. Spodek, B. *Teaching in the Early Years.* 3d ed. Englewood Cliffs, N.J.: Prentice-Hall, 1985.

7. Spodek, B. "Conceptualizing Today's Kindergarten Curriculum." *Elementary School Journal* 89 (1988): 203–11.

8. Teale, W. H., and Sulzby, E. "Emergent Literacy: New Perspectives." In *Emerging Literacy: Young Children Learn to Read and Write,* edited by D. S. Strickland and L. M. Morrow, 1–15. Newark, Del.: International Reading Association, 1989.

9. Wilson, C. R. "Teaching Reading Comprehension by Connecting the Known to the New." *Reading Teacher* 36 (1983): 382–90.

RESOURCES

Bredekamp, S., ed. *Developmentally Appropriate Practice in Early Childhood Programs Serving Children from Birth Through Age 8.* Expanded ed. Washington, D.C.: National Association for the Education of Young Children, 1987.

Brown, J. F. *Curriculum Planning for Young Children.* Washington, D.C.: National Association for the Education of Young Children, 1982.

Eliason, C. F., and Jenkins, L. T. *A Practical Guide to Early Childhood Curriculum.* 3d ed. Columbus, Ohio: Merrill, 1986.

Fountas, I. C., and Hannigan, I. L. "Making Sense of Whole Language: The Pursuit of Informed Teaching." *Childhood Education* 65, no. 3 (1989): 133–37.

Harste, J. C.; Short, K. G.; and Burke, C. *Creating Classrooms for Authors: The Reading-Writing Connection.* Portsmouth, N.H.: Heinemann, 1988.

Hohmann, M.; Banet, B.; and Weikart, D. P. *Young Children in Action.* Ypsilanti, Mich.: High/Scope Press, 1979.

Katz, L. G., and Chard, S. C. *Engaging Children's Minds: The Project Approach.* Norwood, N.J.: Ablex, 1989.

Peterson, K. *Building Curriculum for Young Children: Deciding on Content.* ERIC Document. ED 297886, 1988.

Provenzo, E. F., and Brett, A. *The Complete Block Book.* Syracuse, N.Y.: Syracuse University Press, 1983.

Robison, H., and Spodek, B. *New Directions in the Kindergarten.* New York: Teachers College Press, 1965.

Vacca, J. L.; Vacca, R. T.; and Gove, M. K. *Reading and Learning to Read.* Glenview, Ill.: Scott, Foresman, 1987.

Video: *The Writing Workshop: A World of Difference.* Heinemann Educational Books, 70 Court St., Portsmouth, NH 03801, 603/431-7894.

Bare Books: *Blank Books for Children.* Treetop Publishing, 220 Virginia St., Racine, WI 53405.

5. INTEGRATING MULTICULTURAL PERSPECTIVES INTO EARLY CHILDHOOD EDUCATION

by Min-Ling Tsai

Human beings differ from one another in both their outward appearance and their mental activity. In spite of these differences, I find many similarities between myself and those who at first seemed very different from me. For example, one quiet evening, I heard someone express his needs and longing in prayer. I was surprised that his prayer was much like my own. There are times when human hearts beat as one. One feels common bonds with others when reading a poem or appreciating a film. Our expressions allow us to extend our feelings into human empathy.

In daily life, we seldom reflect on the differences and similarities between ourselves and others. Between moments of hurry and rush, we might pause and think of the fact that people are different. A common attitude might be: "People are different in some ways and similar in others. What's so special about that?" Certainly, we do not want to expose our children to this kind of attitude; neither do we want children to express indifference when interacting with children from other cultural groups. What we want to foster in children's minds, instead, is a multicultural perspective—a way of thinking of people different from ourselves. A multicultural perspective is a vision that transcends the mere recognition of the fact that people are different. It enables us to see and appreciate different viewpoints and feelings, different ways of looking at the world, and at the same time be willing to include, relate to, and cooperate with members of other cultural groups.

As noted in earlier chapters, child development theory and society's cultural values serve as important resources in developing the early childhood education curriculum. The cultural values of American society and its present reality make a multicultural perspective indispensable. The United States is experiencing a pronounced demographic shift. In 1986, Black students comprised 16 percent of the public school population, Hispanics 10 percent, Asians and Pacific Islanders 3 percent, and Native Americans approximately 1 percent. By the turn of the century, about 40 percent of public school students will come from these ethnically diverse backgrounds (3). Thus, multiculturalism is becoming more and more evident in schools across the country. Multiculturalism requires that people in this society learn about other cultures as well as their own. The task of fostering a multicultural perspective is not an option. It is something we must be consciously aware of—something we have to do.

But is it developmentally appropriate to present cultural information to preschool children? Some might argue that the young child's egocentrism and inability to comprehend concepts of time, distance, and symbolism make it difficult to present material on multiculturalism. However, there is much evidence that young children by the age of three are aware of skin color and racial difference (7). Ramsey (4) also points out that we must start with the very young to influence children's basic racial attitudes. Since multiculturalism is a social reality, since children's learning styles are directly influenced by their early childhood experiences, and since preschool children are cognitively able to deal with cultural content, early childhood education must reflect and integrate a multicultural perspective.

Such a perspective can be applied to differences in age, race, class, sex, physical traits and needs, and other human attributes. Here, the discussion will focus only on multiethnic issues. In integrating a multicultural perspective into the early childhood curriculum, we should provide all children with positive cultural identities. At the same time, the children should be aware that different people think in different ways and take different perspectives. They should accept and respect other people's cultures. This is often complicated by stereotypes. Some children associate negative attributes with "things that are different." A recognition of cultural diversity does not mean "tolerance," nor does it mean a move toward the melting away of cultural differences. Rather, children should develop attitudes of acceptance, a respect for differences, and a willingness to communicate with those who are different. To respect means knowing that one's own experiences can be enriched and expanded through the experiences of others. In sum, we hope that children will be willing to relate to, communicate with, and cooperate with persons from other cultures. We hope that this will be a natural part of children's lives.

Since children must recognize cultural diversity as a fact of life, we should help them learn about and communicate with other ethnic groups in a natural and normal fashion. Multiculturalism should be integrated into the curriculum and not be seen as a special subject taught through special activities once or twice a year. Holiday celebrations are an appropriate vehicle, in that they suggest merry, colorful, and appealing activities to children. However, if holidays are the sole or main focus of a multicultural curriculum, they serve only as token gestures (5). Activities that are remote from young children's immediate experiences or that occur with low frequency cannot support meaningful learning for them.

Guidelines for Multicultural Education

In designing an early childhood curriculum with a multicultural perspective, the following guidelines might be helpful:

    1. Multiculturalism embodies an overall perspective rather than a specific curriculum. It should be

integrated into children's everyday experience and infused into every area of the curriculum. Both the arrangement of the physical environment and the design of the activities should reflect cultural diversity. In sum, it should be a natural part of daily learning (2).

2. The multicultural curriculum should reflect each child's unique cultural life pattern. This will allow all children and their parents to feel proud of their culture and also enrich life experiences of other children.

3. Multiculturalism should reflect a commitment to preserve and extend cultural alternatives and broaden the school's cultural base (2). This commitment should be long lasting and not burn out after a fit of enthusiasm.

To implement a multicultural curriculum, teachers should:

1. Create a classroom atmosphere conducive to the recognition of cultural diversity. The physical environment should include storybooks, posters, music, toys, props for dramatic play, and other teaching aids that reflect many cultures.

2. Use parents or other adults of different ethnic groups as resources and experts. Invite them to join discussions on the themes and activities that best depict their life and should therefore be included in the program. Parents can also help to gather materials and resources for the curriculum.

3. Scan the teaching plan for the whole semester or year to find ways to integrate multicultural activities into a

variety of units. The activities should be balanced so that every area of the curriculum has some activities reflecting other cultures. These activities should be designed to complement the total program and facilitate intergroup relations (8). For example, an art project might include paper folding, a Chinese craft, or a project on "the wind" could introduce Chinese kite flying as a normal activity in the project.

Let me use examples from Chinese culture to exemplify how different cultures can be woven into the early childhood curriculum. I have chosen to present this culture and related activities because of my familiarity with it. Many different cultures should be represented in the kindergarten during the year. There is a range of books that can help teachers develop multicultural experiences for young children. These include *The Anti-Bias Curriculum: Tools for Empowering Young Children* (1), *Teaching and Learning in a Diverse World: Multicultural Education for Young Children* (5), and *Understanding the Multicultural Experience in Young Children* (6). The Council on Interracial Books for Children (New York, NY) and ERIC/ EECE (805 West Pennsylvania Avenue, Urbana, IL 61801) can provide information about multicultural resources that are available. Local librarians and representatives of organizations representing minority groups can also help identify resources for children.

INTEGRATING HOLIDAYS AND FESTIVALS INTO EARLY CHILDHOOD EDUCATION

Celebrate a wide variety of holidays and festivals according to the calendar. Although classroom activities should be relatively close to the actual dates of the celebrations, dates are less important than presenting the information in meaningful ways (5). In celebrating the holidays of many groups, all children can feel that their experiences are valued by the whole group.

Ramsey (5) suggests incorporating holidays into the curriculum in terms of their universal themes. Since many parallels exist among holidays of different cultures, this approach provides occasions for children to experience cultural diversity within the context of universals and commonalities.

Descriptions of several Chinese holidays and festivals that can be incorporated into early childhood programs follow.

Chinese New Year

The Chinese New Year, or Spring Festival, is the most important festival in Chinese culture. It is a time to celebrate the birth of the new year, the continuation of life, after surviving the past year.

A long time ago, a monster called "Nien" (meaning "Year") lived deep in the mountain. He came to the village to prey on people, at the end of every year. The village people would hide in their houses or some safe places at this time and came out again the next morning when "Nien" had left. People said "Kung Hsi" (congratulations) to each other for having survived the attack of "Nien."

One time, when "Nien" came down to the village, someone was just putting some dried bamboo sticks into the cooking oven. Knowing the monster was coming near, he ran away without extinguishing the fire. Unexpectedly, "Nien" was frightened away by the "pi-pa" sounds of bamboo cracking in the burning fire.

After this, people used a similar strategy of making loud noises to drive "Nien" away each year. This is one version of the origin of Chinese New Year and the use of firecrackers.

The New Year celebration starts on the thirtieth day of the twelfth moon—New Year's Eve (the Chinese calendar is a lunar calendar). On that evening, family members return home for a family reunion and a splendid feast. Fish, if eaten that day, is not fully consumed, because the character "Yu," meaning fish, is pronounced the same as another "Yu," meaning "to leave something." Hence, fish is saved, meaning that this family has something to be stored every year. After dinner, the children bow to the elders in the family to show their respect. The adults then give them red envelopes containing money.

Since the New Year's season signifies a fresh start, the mood is festive. The home is thoroughly cleaned in preparation and no sweeping is done on New Year's Day, lest the family's good fortune be swept out the door with the dust. No work is done on New Year's Day. The food has been prepared the day before, so that one actually eats last year's food. This is a good omen, signifying one is not so destitute as to have to eat every bit of food as soon as it becomes available. Signs containing couplets to express good wishes and paper guards are pasted on the doors.

In rural China, people spend almost all their time tilling the land. The Chinese New Year season was the only time for them to visit relatives and friends. After a few days' rest, on the fourth or fifth day of the New Year, the sounds of firecrackers proclaim the resumption of business.

Activities

1. *Planting Narcissus Flowers.* The narcissus, which blossoms during the New Year season, is a traditional New Year flower. It is easy for children to plant because all one has to do is place the bulb in a bowl of water filled with pebbles to hold it in place. Growing the narcissus can be an interesting science lesson. Children can compare its attributes with other plants growing in the classroom.

Both the Chinese version of the narcissus story and its Greek version can be told at story time so that children can compare the two stories.

The Chinese Version of the Narcissus Story

A long time ago, in a little village in southern China, there lived an old widow and her only son, A-long. Besides cultivating the land, A-long hunted to make a living.

One day, A-long went hunting early in the morning. The widow found that the rice pot was almost empty. At dusk, the widow washed the small amount of rice left, cooked it, and waited for her son to return home. She grew more and more worried about her son's safety and thought he must be very hungry after hunting all day.

It became darker and darker. The widow pricked up her ears to listen to the sounds of her son's footsteps. After a while, the sounds of footsteps were heard and came closer and clearer. Opening the door, instead of A-long, she found an old, shabbily clothed beggar. He looked weak and spoke to the widow in a tiny voice:

"I am so hungry. Would you please give me some rice or leftovers?"

The widow wanted to help the beggar. But, with only one bowl of rice left, what could she do? "Maybe A-long has killed a big boar today," she thought, and decided to give the only bowl of rice to the beggar.

The rice smelled so good with its rising steam. The old beggar seemed to have hungered for a long, long time for he ate the rice within a few seconds. Licking his mouth clean, he said, "Can I have some more? I am still hungry." Thinking of A-long, who still hadn't come home and had no rice to eat now, the widow shed tears. The old beggar wondered why she cried. After being told by the widow, he felt sorry that he had eaten all their food. He left the widow's house and stood beside the pond nearby. Then, he bent down and spit all the rice he had just eaten into the pond. Then suddenly he disappeared.

After a while, A-long came home with a big, fat hare in his hand. The widow told him about the old beggar. A-long felt that what had happened was quite strange.

The next morning when A-long was ready to go hunting, he passed the pond and was startled by what was beside the pond. The barren land was now filled with white, fragrant, beautiful flowers. The widow came near to look and muttered,

"Is the beggar a god in disguise? Are these flowers transformed by the rice spit from his mouth?"

They named the flowers "water-god" (narcissus). A-long did not go hunting any more. He planted narcissus, sold them, and led a far better life.

2. *Making Chinese New Year Cakes.* See recipe provided at the end of the chapter.

3. *Window paper cutting.* Teachers and children can cut designs from red paper and paste them on the windows. Teachers might be able to find traditional Chinese New Year woodblock prints and window paper decorations to show children the authentic forms and to decorate the classroom. These can also be purchased from China Books and Periodicals (Mail Order Department, 2929 24th St., San Francisco, CA 94110).

4. *Spring Festival Signs.* Teachers can also decorate the classroom with signs (Chun Lien) that they make or they can ask parents to provide some authentic ones.

At New Year time, spring festival signs are pasted on the walls inside the house as well as on the outside of the door.

The most common spring festival sign is a square piece of red paper, with a character signifying "good luck" or "spring." Such signs are usually pasted upside down because "upside down" is pronounced exactly the same as the character "arrive." The upside-down sign expresses the hope that spring and good luck will arrive for the coming year.

Lantern Festival

The fifteenth day of the first moon is the Lantern Festival.

Activities

1. *Cooking Yuan Shiau.* Yuan Shiau are small dumplings eaten on the Lantern Festival.

Recipe

Ingredients: red bean or sesame paste
glutinous rice powder

(These can be bought in a Chinese food mart.)

   a. Take a small portion of red bean paste and roll it into a small ball.
   b. Spread some glutinous rice powder in a pan.
   c. Soak the small ball of red bean paste with water.
   d. Put it into the pan and shake the pan till the ball is covered with glutinous rice powder.
   e. Boil a pot of water and put Yuan Shiau into it.
   f. Boil the Yuan Shiau until they float on the water.

   2. *Making Lanterns.* The traditional Chinese lantern is made of paper and thin bamboo sticks. The one described here is the kind that children in Taiwan make.

   a. Take a can, clean it, and punch two holes on each side. Be sure to watch children carefully for safety's sake.
   b. Cross a piece of wire through the holes.
   c. Fasten the wire on a chopstick, and place a candle into the can. (Setting up the candle in the can is a good topic for a problem-solving discussion.)

   (Children can also make lanterns out of construction paper, but these should not be used with candles.)
   The children can compare Chinese lanterns with pumpkin jack-o-lanterns.

Ching Ming or Grave-Sweeping Festival

   This holiday often falls on April 5th or 6th. On this day, Chinese visit the tombs of their ancestors to show respect to their memory.

April 4—Children's Day in Taiwan

Usually, schools celebrate this holiday with a variety of special programs, such as talent shows, or contests with themes related to children. Parents generally buy gifts for their children on this day.

Dragon Boat Festival

This festival falls on the fifth day of the fifth moon. It is believed that the festival commemorates Chu Yuan, a loyal minister of the king of Chu who committed suicide in the Milo river because his remonstrations had been ignored.

On this day, people eat *tsung tzu* (made mainly of glutinous rice and meat), they make *hsiang pao* (described below), and they hold dragon boat races.

Activities

1. *Making Hsiang Pao.* Hsiang Pao is a small pouch containing incense. It is worn by children during this festival to avoid evil spirits. (See Figure 1.)

2. *Dragon Boat Race.* A small-scale dragon boat festival can be held in the classroom's water table.
   a. If possible, show children pictures of a real dragon boat race in Taiwan or Hong Kong.
   b. The children can make boats either by paper folding or from polystyrene foam.
   c. Separate channels by rope.
   d. Have the children discuss how they can move the boats.
   e. Children can have a race by blowing the boats with straws to see which boat reaches the destination first.

(This activity can be added to projects whose theme is the wind, the boat, or water.)

84

Figure 1
Making Hsiang Pao

Cut the straw apart

Fold a triangle

keep on folding till the end.

Do the same thing with square.

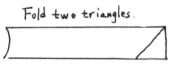

Fold two triangles.

Open it up, make it stand and keep on folding till the end

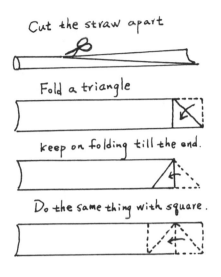

Cut out two pieces of cloth

Sew it up.

Turn it over to hide the seam.

Put the incense bag in and sew up the opening.

Teacher's Day

Confucius is revered as the man who established the system of moral values that has guided the Chinese people from thousands of years ago to the present day in the Republic of China (Taiwan). Out of respect for him as a model teacher, his birthday, which falls on September 28th, is celebrated as Teacher's Day.

OTHER CHINESE ITEMS
FOR THE CLASSROOM

In addition to integrating Chinese holidays and festivals into the early childhood curriculum, the following materials can be included in the classroom:

Snacks: Chinese cookies and desserts, such as pineapple cake, puffed rice cakes, soft flour cakes, tofu cakes, Ma Hua cookies, Chin Hua cookies or sesame peanut cookies. (These items can be bought in a Chinese food mart.)

Block Area: Posters of Chinese architecture (both ancient and modern) can be hung on walls nearby.

Dramatic Play Area: Chinese dolls made of dough, Chinese puppets, paper dolls, Chinese flour people, Chinese opera props such as a whip, or masks of painted faces.

Clay: Chinese play dough.

Art Area: Chinese writing brush, works of calligraphy, and Chinese painting.

Reading Area: Books with Chinese as main characters. For example: Ian Wallace, *Ching Chiang and the Dragon's Dance* (New York: Atheneum, 1984); Diane Wolkstein, *White Wave* (New York: Crowell, 1979); Jane

Yolen, *The Seeing Stick* (New York: Crowell, 1977); and Jane Yolen, *The Emperor and the Kite* (New York: World Publishing, 1967). Unfortunately, few books are available in English that depict modern Chinese.

Musical Instruments: Chinese bells, drums, Chinese flute. (These can be bought in stores in Chinatowns located in such cities as Chicago, Los Angeles, New York, and San Francisco. They may also be available in some local Chinese food stores.

Note: These materials are not just for display. They can be used within suitable unit themes or in appropriate, related activities. For example, a Chinese writing brush can be used by children to experience its feel, which is different from that of a pen. If teachers happen to talk about "written words" of different cultures, resource persons can be invited to demonstrate calligraphy in the classroom.

Chinese Games and Activities

Games Chinese children play can be incorporated into the early childhood education curriculum. They are close to the life experiences of children everywhere. They appeal to children and are developmentally appropriate. In addition, they enhance the development of fine and gross motor skills, creativity, imagination, and cooperation, and are educationally worthwhile. The following activities and games can be allocated in a semester or integrated into any project as long as they match the theme of the project.

Paper Folding

Chinese people love and are very good at using different kinds of paper. A small piece of paper can be folded into a tiny boat, different kinds of hats, a jet plane, a crane, a frog, and other

Figure 2
Paper Folding

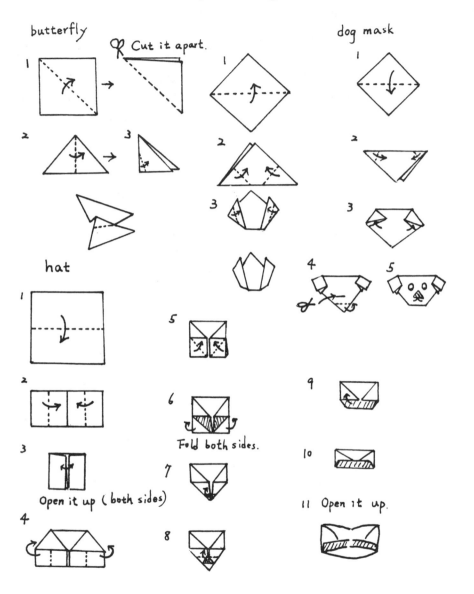

butterfly

Cut it apart.

dog mask

hat

Fold both sides.

Open it up (both sides)

Open it up.

small animals. (See Figure 2.) This activity can enhance fine motor skills and foster children's patience. The products of paper folding can become props in the dramatic play area or can be used to decorate the classroom.

Playing with Rubber Bands

Using one or more rubber bands, children can "pull out" lots of patterns to amuse themselves. This activity enhances the fingers' fine motor development and encourages imagination. It is also appropriate for solitary play. Children can experience elasticity by manipulating the resilient rubber bands. Care needs to be taken in handling rubber bands so that children do not hurt themselves or others.

Many rubber bands can be strung together to form a long jump rope. One child holds each end of the rope while a third child tries to jump over the rope without touching it. The children holding the rope raise the height of the rope gradually, moving it up to the level of the third child's knees, waist, shoulders, mouth, nose, ears, and top of the head. (See Figure 3.)

Chinese Hopscotch

1. Draw a pattern on the ground as shown in Figure 4.

2. At the beginning, throw a marker (a pebble, a small stone, or a bottle cap) into square 1.

3. Players hop on one foot and kick the marker into square 2. Anyone who steps on a line or falls loses the turn and has to start all over again.

4. The first player to reach square 10 is the winner.

5. The winner then chooses a square for a private house and marks it. No one else can stop in the "privately owned house" except the owner. The player with the most private houses wins the game.

89

Figure 3
Playing with Rubber Bands

butterfly

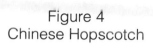

Figure 4
Chinese Hopscotch

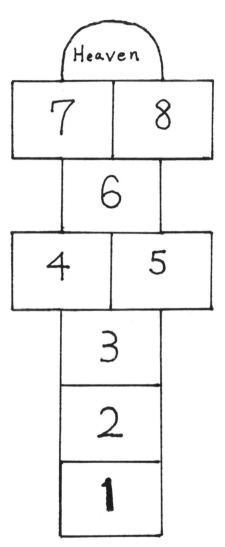

Shadow Figures

This activity can be included in topics related to light, shadow, or hands. The teacher can design hand shadows to illustrate or tell a story. (See Figure 5.) The room should be dark and a blank space on the wall available.

Mask Making

The Chinese people's daily life is closely related to nature. Many of the children's play materials are derived from nature.

1. Use large leaves and flowers to make masks. (It is very possible for spontaneous dramatic play to take place in a field.)

2. The teacher can introduce the names of different plants and their attributes.

3. When children find out that some flowers or leaves stick to their clothes while others do not, it might be a good time to introduce different textures of cloth after returning to the classroom.

Eagle Chases Chicks

This is an outdoor group game played in the yard or playground.

1. Ask a volunteer to be the eagle.

2. Ask one child to be the hen and other children to be chicks. The chicks line up behind the hen, holding their hands tightly on the shoulder or around the waist of the one in front.

3. The game starts with the hungry eagle flying around everywhere to grab the chicks. The hen spreads out her hands as wings to protect her children. The chicks have to run to right or left according to the hen's

Figure 5
Shadow Figures

gesture; at the same time, they have to hold tightly to one another. If a chick gets out of the line, he/she will get caught. This activity reflects the themes that mothers will try every possible way to protect their children and children have to be cooperative in fighting against enemies. It enhances gross motor development and facilitates cooperative learning.

Cooking

Baking Sweet Potatoes. Baking sweet potatoes is a sweet childhood memory for many people who grew up in Taiwan. Since food is a topic dear to almost all children, exploring the taste of baked sweet potatoes might provide an excellent beginning for learning about cultural differences.

Making New Year's Cake

Ingredients:
6 cups glutinous rice powder
2 cups sugar (either white or brown)
2 cups water
cellophane, 12 inches in diameter
bamboo basket for steaming food

These ingredients can be bought in a local Chinese food mart.

1. Stir sugar in water until completely dissolved.
2. Pour glutinous rice powder in mixture and stir it well.
3. Spread the cellophane in the bamboo basket.
4. Pour the sugar and rice mixture into the basket and steam for two hours.

Many Chinese utensils are made of natural materials, such as bamboo. Many Chinese desserts are steamed in bamboo baskets so as to imbue the food with the refreshing smell of bamboo.

Teachers can introduce the Chinese way of making cakes, which is different from the Western way (steaming versus baking).

Chinese eat New Year's cake at New Year festivals. It is pronounced *Nien* (year) *Gou* (cake). Eating New Year's cake symbolizes good luck because the pronunciation suggests being promoted higher and higher every year.

EVALUATING THE MULTICULTURAL PROGRAM

Evaluating the multicultural aspects of the curriculum is more problematic than it is for other areas of the kindergarten program. Generally we can evaluate programs and their outcomes by observing the children and analyzing their work to determine what they have learned. We usually make our judgment based upon immediate observations.

We can do the same with the multicultural program. We can use direct observations, checklists, rating scales, and the techniques discussed in other chapters of this publication to determine what the children have learned. This information will give us a fairly reliable estimate of what the children have come to know. Such information, however, can only give us an assessment of the superficial aspects of the multicultural curriculum. While knowledge and appreciation of a variety of cultures are important outcomes of the program, there are deeper goals that should concern us.

Multicultural education is important as a vehicle to help children learn to understand, accept, and value persons from cultures other than their own. The sense of appreciation that we hope will result from such a program and the attitudes and values we wish young children to gain will show up in many different ways, some of which we cannot anticipate. Several of these will not be evident for some time to come. Thus possibly the most important outcomes of the multicultural curriculum are the hardest to evaluate. We may be able to find only indirect indicators that the children have achieved the goals we desire and it may take a great deal of sensitivity and attention on the part of the teacher to identify these. Nevertheless, the multicultural curriculum is a valuable part of kindergarten. It reflects some of the most basic values of our society. Even without adequate evaluation it is important to include this in the kindergarten program and to seek the best ways we can to determine how successful we are in achieving the understandings, values, and attitudes we wish to see in children as they interact with peers and adults who seem different and who come from backgrounds that are different from theirs.

REFERENCES

1. Derman-Sparks, L. *The Anti-Bias Curriculum: Tools for Empowering Young Children.* Washington D.C.: National Association for the Education of Young Children, 1989.
2. Mock, K. "Integrating Multiculturalism in Early Childhood Education from Theory to Practice." In *Multicultural Education Programmes and Methods,* edited by R. J. Samuda and S. L. Kong. Toronto: University of Toronto Press, 1986.
3. Ramirez, B. A. "Culturally and Linguistically Diverse Children." *Teaching Exceptional Children* 20, no.4 (1988): 45–51.
4. Ramsey, P. G. "Multicultural Education in Early Childhood." *Young Children* 37 (1982): 13–23.
5. ____. *Teaching and Learning in a Diverse World: Multicultural Education for Young Children.* New York: Teacher's College Press, 1987.
6. Saracho, O. N., and Spodek, B. *Understanding the Multicultural Experience in Young Children.* Washington D.C.: National Association for the Education of Young Children, 1983.
7. Swadener, E. B. "Implementation of Education That Is Multicultural in Early Childhood Settings: A Case Study of Two Day-Care Programs." *Urban Review* 20, no.1 (1988): 8–26.
8. New York State Education Department. *A Multicultural Early Childhood Resource Guide.* ERIC Document Reproduction Service No. ED 280924, 1987.

6. CREATING MEANINGFUL KINDERGARTEN PROGRAMS

by Mary Gatzke

Kindergarten is not just a year of preparation for first grade. It is a unique and valuable educational experience in itself. It is a segment of the child's education to be lived and celebrated to the fullest. The richness and quality of the experiences encountered in kindergarten contribute to the child's development as a lifelong learner with each stage important and contributing (2). Since kindergarten is one of the earliest stages in a child's education, schools should use the opportunity to impact on children. The curriculum should provide the foundation of an educational structure that will grow as tall and strong as possible.

In creating a meaningful kindergarten curriculum, teachers should be guided by three principles:

1. Provide learning experiences within meaningful contexts.

2. Challenge children's thinking abilities through the experiences offered to them.

3. Go beyond developmentally appropriate.

This chapter explores each of these ideas.

PROVIDE LEARNING EXPERIENCES WITHIN MEANINGFUL CONTEXTS

We know that young children experience and learn about their world as unified whole experiences, rather than in segregated subject matter areas such as science or social studies (4). When kindergarten teachers present concepts out of their normal, meaningful context and teach them as isolated ideas, they make it harder for children to understand them. While most adults can understand decontextualized concepts and principles, young children have a more difficult time with such learning.

For example, to teach young children concepts about their five senses, a teacher could devote one week of activities to smelling, another week to tasting, a third to matching textures, a fourth to discriminating shapes and colors, and a final week to identifying sounds. All the senses will get "covered" in this way. But, at the end of the five weeks, will the children know anything about the senses they didn't know at the beginning of the first week? Will they be able to put their new forms of discrimination and their new vocabulary to use as they experience their world? Chances are, they will not.

It is probable that more valuable learning will occur if the children use their senses in naturally occurring situations and try to draw meanings from what they have experienced. For example, they can smell and taste the peanut butter at snack time and compare it to the honey they had yesterday. The children could see if they can find the bird they hear in the playground, not only identifying the sound, but the source of the sound as well, and deciding if the feather they found could have come from that bird, matching color and texture. These are real learning problems embedded in natural context with sensory discrimination—in this case auditory and visual—waiting to be discovered within them. Only suggestions from a skilled teacher are required to focus the children's attention and turn these potential learning opportunities into meaningful learning experiences.

Another example of using sensory perception to answer meaningful questions is to make decisions about what to wear for going outdoors. Finding out if the wind is blowing by observing tree branches, a flag, or smoke from chimneys tells you beforehand if you will need a jacket or hood. Reluctance to wear boots or zip coats on rainy or snowy days can be dealt with by comparing drops of water on materials from which shirts, jeans, and tennis shoes are made with materials from which coats, mittens, and boots are made. Such observations can lead to judgments about which should be used for umbrellas, raincoats, or towels.

CHALLENGE CHILDREN'S THINKING ABILITIES

Young children need to be provided with activities that require thinking, and that encourage questioning and wondering. Some kindergarten activities limit the degree to which children can get involved. While such activities may be developmentally appropriate, they become ritualistic and offer little intellectual challenge to children. If activities do not challenge children's thinking, they may not be educative even though they use concrete manipulative materials, are based on firsthand experiences, and are child-initiated.

There are other ways of teaching kindergarten children about the senses. Rather than repeating the experiences and understandings that children already know, the teacher should move them to new levels of thought. A teacher, for example, could ask the children if people's eyes are similar to or different from those of animals. They could look at pets at home or at school, at animals in the zoo, or at pictures of animals. They could compare the size, shape, location, number, parts, and colors of eyes in the various animals as well as the eyes of the different children in the class. Questions like the following could be used to focus their explorations:

- Which animals have eyes that are bigger or smaller than ours?

- Do any animals have more than two eyes, less than two?

99

- Do animals have eyelids?

- How do eyelids work? What purpose do you think they serve?

- How many different colors of eyes can you find in our classroom?

- What colors are the different animals' eyes?

- Are all animals' eyes on the front of their head like ours are? If they're in a different place, do they see different things than we do?

Another opportunity for challenging children's thinking is offered by a bird's nest. In addition to knowledge gained from seeing, touching, feeling, and holding the nest, children can be stimulated to discover information about birds. These experiences can lead to connections in children's minds between this nest and their environment.

- What kinds of things is the nest made from?

- Where would a bird have found the scrap of plastic bread sack, the fishing line, the horsehair, the piece of red yarn, or the candy wrapper?

- Which materials did the bird use most? Least?

- How are the materials held together?

- What do people use instead of mud to make something stick together?

- What materials do people use to weave? What do they make from weaving?

- What tools or parts of its body did the bird use to make this nest?

- Are all bird nests made from the same things?

These questions offer many possibilities for extending children's understandings within a meaningful context.

GO BEYOND DEVELOPMENTALLY APPROPRIATE

Developmental appropriateness has become widely accepted as the criterion for creating or selecting programs for young children (1). It suggests that the level of difficulty of an activity and the method of instruction used should match the ability levels and learning styles of the children. But before you select an activity or decide how to teach something, you need to select what you are going to teach and why. Developmental appropriateness suggests only the match of ability level and method, the "how" of the program (5). No indication is given of what the content should be or how it should be selected: the "what" and "why" of the program. At the same time as teachers judge the developmental appropriateness of activities, they should judge the educational appropriateness of the activities:

- Is the concept taught worth knowing by kindergarten children?

- Are there situations where it will be useful to them?

- Will it help them solve problems in their daily experiences?

- Will knowing this concept help children participate in and contribute to their society in some meaningful way? (6)

If these questions are answered positively and there is a positive assessment of developmental appropriateness, then the activities should be included in the curriculum (7).

There are no universal answers to these questions. The answers depend upon the unique experience and background of each particular group of children. Lobster pots and bait buckets may be everyday materials in the lives of children from a New England coastal fishing community, but may be exotica to midwest farm children for whom combines and silage are part of their daily experience. It might be educationally inappropriate to teach about seashores and tidal pools to kindergarten children who live a thousand miles from the ocean and have never seen it. Lessons on subways and monorails might be beyond rural and small town children who have not experienced mass transit systems. Lessons on horses and cows might be meaningless to children in rural Alaska who know instead about the seals, salmon, and foxes of their environment. Children who have always known the freedom and spaciousness of living on a farm may not understand the confinement of apartment living or the need to have to go to a park to play.

For one group of young children whose classroom was located near a high school track and practice field, finding out about track and field events was educationally appropriate. The children could see the high school athletes practicing on the field and became interested in what they were doing. A class trip to the track to talk with the athletes provided firsthand information. Guided by the tenets of educational appropriateness (i.e., worth knowing, usefulness, helpful in problem solving and participating in society), the teacher brought this experience back into the classroom. Opportunities were provided for children to use their new vocabulary, try out new roles, and experiment with new ideas.

The children replicated and tried out each event, complete with vocabulary, required equipment, and physical skills. Finding appropriate locations for running, jumping, and throwing events required planning and a concern for safety. The children constructed equipment such as cardboard hurdles and made suitable substitutions, such as a bamboo pole for a javelin, a frisbee for a discus, and a nerf ball for a shot. Chalk lines drawn on the sidewalk provided practice staying in one's own lane while

This experience presented an excellent opportunity for developing concepts of measurement. Some events, like races, are measured in units of time. Others are measured in units of distance—either the length of a throw or the height of a jump. Different instruments are used for each kind of measurement. Stop watches and clocks measure time. Yardsticks measure short distances; tape measures, longer ones. All measurements are in numbers. For distance measurements, the biggest number wins because that is the farthest. For time measurements, the smallest number wins because that is the fastest.

Another type of numeration was encountered in winning. Winners are ranked by order—first, second, third. Different ranks receive different colored ribbons as prizes. Many opportunities were found for practicing reading and writing numbers as well: individual competitors' numbers worn on their backs, coaches'clipboards to keep track of scores and measurements, numbered running lanes, and place numbers on winners' ribbons.

The children had to develop the concept of what a team is and the social skills needed to be a team member: a team has many members; each member has a different job but all members work to help each other; teams have a coach who is their leader or teacher; team members help each other practice so they can become better at what they do; teams have a team name and team colors; all team members wear uniforms that are their team colors. The children had to decide on a team name and colors for their class team. They even designed a team T-shirt for their uniform.

Every community has a local high school, college, or professional athletic team of some sort. Connecting this concept to the community can be easily accomplished. Identifying teams by their uniforms, colors, and team names encourages visual discrimination and print awareness.

Sports events change with the seasons so such a project

could continue throughout the year. Variety in regional and local emphasis should be considered. Sports like hockey, skiing, and rodeos are the center of some communities and nonexistent in others. In Olympic years, extending the project to include either the summer or winter Olympics might be relevant. Including Special Olympics builds understanding of handicaps and differences in ability that need to be considered. It also can help children understand that there are different valid levels of competition.

Learning about track and field events can be brought into the classroom in many ways besides dramatic play and large motor activities. Adding accessories to unit block play may encourage construction of a small-scale track. Small people figures, paper squares and tape to make number signs for them, string for a finish line, plastic chips for discus, foam scraps for a high jump pad are a few possibilities. Learning also could be extended through teacher-made card or lotto games matching events and ways to measure scores (i.e., race with stop watch) or classifying events as throwing, running, or jumping (i.e., race, hurdles, and relay = running) or matching equipment to events (i.e., finish line = race, sand pit = broad jump). The art materials could be used to design team uniforms or create a mural depicting two teams competing in various events. At the water table, possible water events could be devised such as swim races, diving, and rowing, along with methods to measure performance. The teacher could add new events, such as potato sack races, or devise others that require partners such as leap frog, wheelbarrow races, and water balloon tosses to develop skills in working together.

COMBINING PRINCIPLES FOR MEANINGFUL CURRICULUM

The following example compares the approaches of two kindergarten teachers to the same lesson. One teacher used the three guidelines suggested in selecting educational experiences for the children; the other did not. Columbus Day is an important event and part of our cultural heritage; learning about this historical event should be included in the kindergarten curriculum. These teachers presented the holiday to their children in different ways. Very different learnings resulted.

The first teacher read a book about Christopher Columbus to her class. The book selected was age-appropriate in every way, including vocabulary level, amount of information included, attractive pictures, and length of story. The teacher's presentation was excellent. She explained concepts, defined new words, asked questions to involve the children in an active learning situation, and reviewed major ideas in a group discussion after the book was read. Following this whole group activity, the children could select a followup activity from the choices provided: playing with sailboats at the water table, making boats from clay with toothpick and paper sails, and coloring in pictures of Columbus and his ship.

While these activities meet all the criteria for developmental appropriateness and were designed to develop specific skills such as coloring within lines, or cutting and gluing, they are not very generative. They did not do much to develop and extend the children's understanding of Columbus's feat of discovery. They provided no sense of history to the children or no understanding of what it meant to travel many months in a small boat over uncharted waters.

The second teacher began her lesson on Columbus by reading the same book. Her presentation was similar to that of the first teacher and she also used a group discussion to check for understanding of the concepts presented. However, she followed the discussion with the suggestion, "I wonder if we could build the Santa Maria in our classroom? What would we need to do?" Children immediately offered ideas and volunteered for specific tasks. Soon the room was full of small groups of children, each working on some part of the building project. Some were hauling the large blocks out to the center of the room where others were arranging them using their newly learned vocabulary of terms like bow, stern, and hold. Another group was locating a mop handle to use as the mast and deciding whether to use doll blankets or newspaper for the sails. The ship's steering wheel was being constructed from tinker toys and cardboard tubes anchored to a box. The flag group had found a picture of the flag of Spain in the encyclopedia and was selecting appropriate colored markers to recreate it. The ship's name group was finding out where the name went and what letters would be needed to make "Santa Maria." Another group was stapling together pieces of paper and carefully printing the date across each page of the captain's log. A paper towel tube was being turned into a spyglass and stars were being hung overhead to guide the voyage. The supply of dress-up clothes was searched for sailors' bandannas, berets, and long vests for the captain. Jump ropes became rigging and sandpails and coffee cans became buckets for swabbing the decks. Still other children packed supplies and food into trunks and barrels to be stored in the hold. The suggestion of fishing resulted in the ocean surrounding the ship being filled with an assortment of fish, whales, sharks, and octopi.

For several days America was discovered and redis-covered. Everyone had the opportunity to be Columbus guiding his ship, the sailors adjusting the sails, and the mate looking through the spyglass shouting, "Land Ahead!" Snacks of pilot bread and water were relished when eaten in the cabin. The spirit of adventure—not unlike that felt by the original crew—was recreated in this classroom by providing opportunities to become genuinely involved in learning.

Certainly the pursuit of learning in this manner requires that children have some skills and prior knowledge, for freedom requires competence (6). The freedom of exploration and inquiry is dependent upon competence in the skills of investigation and a knowledge base to work from (which for young children is very limited). A delicate balance must be maintained between children's explorations and teachers' interventions, for one cannot expand without the other. But a teacher's belief in children as competent learners who actively seek knowledge must be demonstrated, not just stated in the program philosophy. There must be a very conscious awareness of the degree to which the curriculum offers true challenges to children's understandings and extends them to new levels of learning.

For the Columbus project described above, the children's learning need not be limited to this one activity centering around a holiday. Learning tasks can be open-ended, providing opportunities for extension beyond the topic at hand. For example, an interest in flags that might develop from making the flag of Spain could be extended to study flags of different countries or how flags are used in a community. A walking field trip looking for different kinds of flags could follow. Learning that could result includes understanding that clubs, states, countries, teams, schools, and cities have flags that represent them. Flags have designs or symbols that often tell something about the organization they represent. There are rules for displaying flags. Some flags are triangle-shaped, others are rectangles. Different kinds of flags are used for special purposes. Construction workers signal traffic to slow down with flags. Waving a flag can start or stop a race. Warning flags are placed on long boards that stick out behind a truck.

Interest in the spyglass used on the play ship and the stars and compass for navigation could lead to examining telescopes. The children could also learn about such constellations as the Big Dipper, and even visit a planetarium, if one is available in the community.

Eating pilot bread or crackers may lead to questions of what would happen to fresh bread or fruit after several days on a ship. The children could experiment with putting bread in a large sealed jar and observing it over succeeding days or weeks. This could lead to a new understanding of the purpose of refrigerators or the use of drying or other forms of preserving foods.

Writing events in the captain's log may create interest in keeping diaries and journals. This could lead to the class developing its own journals, either dictated to the teacher, or kept by individual children, depending on their ability levels. Using the calendar to keep track of time is another activity that could develop from the study of Columbus and his journey.

New vocabulary and an evolving understanding of the parts of ships may result in more intricate construction of boats in blockbuilding or woodworking. Experimenting with sails of different materials, different sizes and shapes of sailboats that are raced in the water table or on a pond would lead to increased understanding of wind, resistance, speed, and balance.

Such activities are not without opportunities for social and emotional growth as well. Assuming the role of captain, fulfilling the responsibilities of a sailor, or experiencing the crowded quarters in the cabin can teach such social skills as turn-taking, sharing, and empathy for others.

THE TEACHER AS THE CRITICAL DIFFERENCE

The contrast in opportunities for meaningful learning between these two classrooms is evident. The critical factor that made the difference in how the two programs evolved was not the facilities, the equipment, the time, or the children—all of which are often cited as obstacles to providing high-quality kindergarten programs. The difference was the teacher—one kindergarten teacher saw curriculum opportunities in an annual event that might have been treated as merely ritual; the other let the curriculum dictate the events to her.

Creating meaningful curriculum requires seeing opportunities as potential learning experiences and valuing the process of learning (i.e., children as thinkers and decision makers) over the product. It means believing that children encounter the world as a unified whole and structuring the curriculum in the same manner, replacing projects that are not projects at all but participation in teacher-initiated lessons with predetermined knowledge to be learned (3). Above all, it means teaching children to value their ideas as well as the teacher's ideas and to support children in their learning rather than direct it.

REFERENCES

1. Bredekamp, S. *Developmentally Appropriate Practices.* Washington, D.C.: National Association for the Education of Young Children, 1986.

2. Elkind, D. "Early Childhood Education on Its Own Terms." In *Early Schooling: The National Debate,* edited by S. L. Kagan and E. Zigler. New Haven: Yale University Press, 1987.

3. Humphrey, S. "Becoming a Better Kindergarten Teacher: The Case of Myself." *Young Children* 44, no. 6 (1989): 17–21.

4. Krogh, S. *The Integrated Early Childhood Curriculum.* New York: McGraw-Hill, 1990.

5. Spodek, B. "What Are the Sources of Early Childhood Curriculum?" In *Early Childhood Education,* edited by B. Spodek, 81–91. Englewood Cliffs, N.J.: Prentice Hall, 1973.

6. ____. "What Constitutes Worthwhile Educational Experiences for Young Children." In *Teaching Practices: Reexamining Assumptions,* edited by B. Spodek, 5–20. Washington, D.C.: National Association for the Education of Young Children, 1976.

7. ____. "Development, Values and Knowledge in the Kindergarten Curriculum." In *Today's Kindergarten: Exploring the Knowledge Base, Expanding the Curriculum,* edited by B. Spodek, 32–47. New York: Teachers College Press, 1986.

8. ____. "Conceptualizing Today's Kindergarten Curriculum." *Elementary School Journal,* 89, no. 2 (1988): 203–11.

THE CONTRIBUTORS

Patricia Clark Brown is a doctoral student in early childhood education at the University of Illinois at Urbana-Champaign. Earlier she was a teacher of bilingual children in the Boston public schools and the director of a child care center. Her research interests are in the areas of curriculum and teaching in early childhood education.

Mary Gatzke is an assistant professor specializing in early childhood education at the University of Wyoming. She is a former primary grade teacher in Montana and a teacher in the Head Start programs of Montana and Alaska.

Jeanette Allison Hartman is an assistant professor specializing in early childhood education at Indiana University of Pennsylvania. She has served as program advisor for Fresno County (California) Head Start, as editorial assistant for the *Early Childhood Research Quarterly,* and as a teacher of young children.

Melanie Turnipseed Kenney is a kindergarten teacher in the Urbana (Illinois) public schools, working with at-risk children. She has taught prekindergarten, kindergarten, and primary classes in a number of schools. She has also served as program consultant to schools and has presented workshops at state and national meetings of teachers.

Bernard Spodek is Professor of Early Childhood Education at the University of Illinois at Urbana-Champaign. He has also taught nursery, kindergarten, and elementary classes. His research and scholarly interests are in the areas of curriculum, teaching, and teacher education in early childhood education. Dr. Spodek has lectured extensively in the United States,

Australia, Canada, China, England, Israel, Japan, Mexico, and Taiwan. He is a former president of the National Association for the Education of Young Children, and chair of the Early Education and Child Development Special Interest Group of the American Educational Research Association. He is the author and/or editor of numerous works in the field of early childhood education.

Min-Ling Tsai is a doctoral student in early childhood education at the University of Illinois at Urbana-Champaign. A native of Taiwan, she is a former teacher of English in a junior high school in Taipei.